Following My Father's Dreams

To order additional copies, please contact us.
BookSurge, LLC
www.booksurge.com
1-866-308-6235
orders@booksurge.com

Following My Father's Dreams

JOURNALS FROM A ROOKIE IDITAROD RUN

James and Christopher Warren

2005
www.warren-enterprises.com

Following My Father's Dreams

Table of Contents

A Few Words From the Author:

It didn't start out this way. I had no intent to write a book, ever. I hadn't a clue of the strong infuences of a father. But hindsight is a blessing.

My father, Al Warren, was a disabled war veteran. He never complained of his handicap and beat the odds to live well beyond the predictions. He couldn't do the physical things other men enjoyed. But his dreams of Alaska and his habit of giving me books and articles after he had finished reading, made a lasting impact on me. Perhaps his hard-headed Scottish work ethic played a role too.

The message is simple but powerful. Fathers, your influence on your children is much bigger than you will ever know. Use it wisely.

This book is a tribute to my father's influence. I am sure it would come as a complete surprise to him.

Jim Warren

In Appreciation:

Attorney by day, wife, mother and sled dog care giver by night, Jennifer is the spark that created this book. Thinking outside the box, she saw the possibility and pulled together the first draft while Chris, the dogs, and I were still on the trail. Thank you, Jennifer, for your 'possibility thinking'.

Jennifer has found ways to connect to the dogs in ways the rest of the family has not. She says, "Their wagging tails and smiling faces are my therapy after a long hard day." She claims the dogs always give back more than they are given. Maybe that is why she spends many hours in the dog yard, petting, brushing, and generally loving the dogs.

On behalf of Christopher, Whitney, and all the dogs, thanks Jennifer. We appreciate you.

Jim

Jennifer with Hartley and Swen

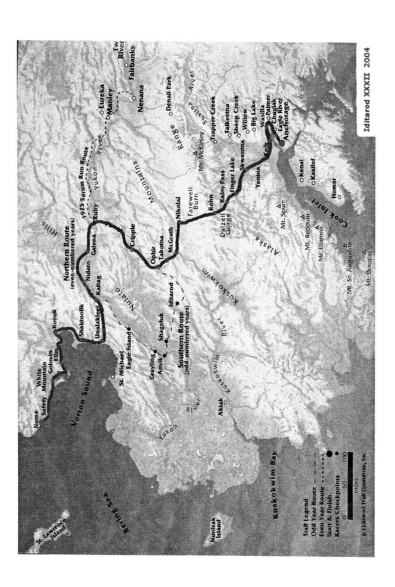

Iditarod XXXII 2004

Twin
River
Fairbanks

Eureka
Manley
Nenana

Denali Park

Yukon River

Koyukuk River

Range

Mountains

1925 Serum Run Route

Ruby

Northern Route
(even-numbered years)

Galena

Nulato

Kaltag

Nulato

Cripple

Ophir
Takotna

McGrath

Nikolai

Farewell
Burn

Rohn

Dalzell
Gorge

Rainy Pass

Finger Lake

Skwentna

Yentna

Knik

Mt. McKinley

Susitna River

Trapper Creek

Talkeetna

Sheep Creek

Willow

Big Lake

Wasilla

Palmer
Chugiak
Eagle River
Anchorage

Mt. Spurr

Mt. Redoubt

Mt. Iliamna

Mt. St. Augustine

Mt. Douglas

Kenai

Kasilof

Homer

Cook Inlet

Alaska

Kuskokwim

Iditarod

Shageluk

Anvik

Grayling

St. Michael

Eagle Island

Unalakleet

Shaktoolik

Koyuk

Elim

Golovin

White
Mountain

Safety

Nome

Norton Sound

Southern Route
(odd-numbered years)

Kuskokwim River

Aklak

Yukon River

Hills

Bering Sea

St. Lawrence
Island

Nunivak
Island

Kuskokwim Bay

Trail Legend
Odd Year Route
Even Year Route
Start & Finish
Racers Checkpoints

miles
0   50   100

(c) Iditarod Trail Committee, Inc

Jennifer's Introduction

My maiden name is Swenson. The year Jim Warren and I got married, Rick Swenson (no relation as far as I can tell) won his second Iditarod. Jim and I were racing in the SCCA PRO Rally circuit at the time and he said something about how great it would be to run the Iditarod some day. We were used to taking risks, but I thought the Iditarod sounded a bit extreme. Besides, all we had was a golden retriever

Some 18 years later, we were headed to Michigan's Upper Peninsula and came across a little store, Tun-Dra Outfitters, whose owner ran adventure tours. We signed up for a three-week Iditarod tour, and had a great time. The whole while, however, Jim kept comparing the race to our rally car experience, and talked about using dogs to promote our Christmas tree farm. That summer we bought nine "recreational" dogs. Three were from a Michigan musher who had attempted the Iditarod, and six were from champion Jeff King. We figured it would be better to buy dogs that knew more than we did. The kids were thrilled, especially our daughter, Whitney. She and her brother Chris became determined to become mushers along with Jim. We joined the local club, Mid-Union Sled Haulers (M.U.S.H) to learn more. We ran some races.

Our kennel grew. We went back to Alaska for a summer trip. We bought "mid-distance" dogs, some from Jeff King again, and some from Linwood Fiedler, who had finished 2nd in the 2001 Iditarod. One of Jeff's dogs, Ruby had been bred to Beta, whom we were also buying, and we had puppies. This was something I had been totally and emphatically against, until they showed up. We ran more races. Jim bought me a sled, hoping to get me hooked on sledding, as well. It looked suspiciously like a Kenny Hess sled that he had purchased the year before, for long distance.

In 2002, Jim called Jeff again and said he needed faster leaders, and that he was looking to run long distance. More dogs arrived. We had another litter. I was in love with more puppies. We sold some of the earlier dogs. We bought dogs from Bob and Jan Shaw, who were reducing their kennel size, and had been winning races in the Midwest for years. We talked about Jim running the Iditarod someday, but thought he should try a few more seasons racing, first. The 2002 and 2003 seasons were not stellar, but we were getting experience. Then some friends talked Jim into going for it. When his mom became gravely ill, he decided that he wasn't getting any younger himself.

While training for the 2004 Iditarod, Jim decided to keep journals and post them on our rough, but functional web site. At first the entries were scattered over the weeks; then, as he trained he started writing more often. Friends started reading and commenting. When we finally decided to enter the race, our website was included in the entrant information. More people started to read about Jim's adventures with the dogs. We got e-mails, and an AP reporter called. Did we know that Jim would be the oldest rookie to run this year? Our son Chris graduated from high school early and started to write as well. More e-mails came.

There didn't seem to be much out there describing the Iditarod from the perspective of a rookie and his family.

The web page was too hard to print for most people; so here is the collection of journals and some of the e-mails that we received during this time. The pictures are a mix from Chris, me, and Chris's traveling companions, Charlie Eshbach and Andy Klevorn. We hope you enjoy.

Deciding to go

Jim, April 30, 2003: This last weekend at a potluck dinner at Lloyd and Mary Gilbertson's, Lloyd asked me when I was planning to run in the Iditarod. After some discussion he pointed out that I could get the final qualifier I needed in December and that it would be no additional burden in conditioning the dogs. In fact it would force an early start in dog training. That got me thinking! Maybe this should be the year? Jennifer seems to be supportive but isn't turning somersaults at the idea. Chris will be able to finish high school in January and could be the handler? Maybe?

I came from my annual medical physical today. I told the Doc I was planning on running the Iditarod. Other than some aching and stiff joints and feeling tired when I am working hard, I had no other real complaints. He gave me a completely clean bill of health; a heart like a man in his 20s, ailments related to a steady stressful job gone. He did advise me to document my efforts to running the Iditarod! He thought it would be great for my daughter to show her children and friends 20 years from now. The implication was that I may be dead by then but I quickly dismissed the thought. On his advice I will begin taking notes. They will contain as much of the picture as I can capture. Maybe somebody will enjoy or better yet gain insight or encouragement from them. So here we go!

Driving home from Dr. Nadolski's office I am somewhat overwhelmed by the amount that must get done before

March of '04. Dogs to train, cabin to get up to speed, Christmas trees to farm and sell, family things, finances... So I'll get started the only way I know how... START!

I went to Lowe's Home Improvement Center and stood in the electrical aisle and engineered the electrical distribution system for the cabin. I'll let the design set in my head overnight and buy the stuff tomorrow for installation next weekend. But how can I do electrical work and train the dogs too, there are only so many hours in the day. Streamline, that's how. I'll take fewer dogs, and be sure I have all the materials to do the electrical work. Perhaps, I could leave on Sunday, a day earlier just to be sure it all can get done.

Jim, May 6: The electrical at the cabin is done. So, after running the dogs, I traveled on the quad 45 miles to the Whitefish Point area north of the cabin scouting out trails for dog training. What beautiful country. I stopped the quad to look at my maps and GPS when I heard a partridge drumming so near it sounded like it was sitting on my lap. What a beautiful sight. I've never seen one drumming so close.

Sitting there on the quad I began thinking about where did this Iditarod stuff start with me. It is so much more than a sled dog race. Is it the freedom, the space, the adventure? Is it being alone on the trail with my dogs, at peace? I think it started when I was about 10 or 12 when Dad handed me a book titled White Fang by Jack London. He gave me every other book by Jack London after he finished. It struck me many years later that Dad read every dog and Alaska book ever written. I noticed the ones he had on his shelf were badly worn from reading. The Bible was the only thing he read more. It also struck me that he followed the Alaskan homesteaders in detail and he often told stories of what he had read. Yes, I believe he dreamed of Alaska, and of having a healthy body so he could go and see it for himself. But he didn't. He never saw the northern lights crackling overhead. He never saw the salmon in the streams, the mountains, the wolves, Denali at dawn, or Unalakleet with 80 MPH winds. He never saw the sled dogs with 1100 miles in 10 days come trotting into Nome, and he never saw daylight at midnight. But I know he dreamed about it, and his dream infected me.

So where does it end? I don't know or care. In the mean time, it is a great a ride.

Fall Training

Jim, September 8: After enduring summer with too much to do, things are ready! I just came in from the new dog yard at SledDog Lodge and there is much enthusiasm. The temperature is dropping through 50 degrees and in the morning it will be our first serious run of the training season. The dogs know and are excited. The excitement is infectious. I can hardly wait and think it would be fun to hook up and run tonight while it is cool.

Moe, the veteran of several Iditarods, is so excited he is jumping around as much as the pups. Bingo, he is 8 too, has been acting like a puppy ever since the weather began to cool a month ago. They both will have a shot a making the 18 dogs I'll take to Alaska. I hope they make it. Their experience might be vital, especially when things get tough.

When thinking of the race, I am sobered by the thought of storms. I understand there is nothing like a coastal storm when visibility drops to near zero. All one can do is hunker down and try to wait it out. I've been in Unalakleet on the sea coast and for two full days the wind was a sustained 40-50 mph gusting to 70-80. Visibility in the village was about 100 feet. Life functions normally there under such conditions. Is there something we could learn? I hope we have a couple of storms here to practice our survival skills. We had one blizzard during last years training that was so bad I nearly had to stop. I thought we had gotten off the trail. I hoped the dogs knew where the trail was. I didn't.

We went through some 6 foot drifts, dropped onto a bare wind swept section of trail and behold, underneath us were dog tracks we had made hours earlier. I just trusted them for the rest of the way home.

In a race like the Iditarod if you come up missing, they will send someone out looking for you. During training, nobody knows you are out, much less knows where to look. Things are more risky during training.

Well, it is time to finish my training plan. With so many dogs, 39, I have to make a couple of cuts to ensure I have time to train all of my dogs adequately. I'd like to have 2000 miles on them before we head for Alaska. That will be a challenge!

Jim, About Dog training: Our philosophy for training is to keep the dogs healthy and enthusiastic about running. To accomplish this we start early in the fall with runs of 2-3 miles and gradually ramp up the mileage taking care to not expect too much before weather cools. Plus we always run toward food and a warm bed and insert ample days off. The dogs may run 3-5 consecutive days then get a 1-3 day break. After 20-25 mile runs are attained, trail camping including equal time for run and rest is used to stretch miles. Once 40-50 mile continuous runs are attained, back to back runs with equal rests between are used to get the dogs into the run-rest mode. Late in the training season, some training runs are as much as 200 overall miles taking 2-3 days. The dogs run in all types of weather to acclimate them to different conditions so long as it poses no health risk.

Our training camp is located 10 miles North of Tahquamenon Falls near the Lake Superior shore in Michigan's Upper Peninsula. We call it SledDog Lodge. The nearest neighbor is 3 miles away. There are hundreds of miles of ideal dog training trails

Resting on the Trail

Chris, September 9: With school in full swing now, I have decided my father really is slightly crazy. This isn't a new revelation, more of a confirmation of my suspicions. After all, I can't even begin to count the number of stories he's told that left me shaking my head. Now he is training for the Iditarod.

The days are cool enough now at our cabin that I rarely see him for more than two or three days. That being the case, I find that I am doing more and more to keep the family running on top of my school work; groceries, cooking, laundry, yard work, the whole lot. If I did a task before, it seems that I do it more frequently and with less help.

School this year is interesting to say the least. I only have two of what I call "real" classes. They are AP English and AP Calculus BC (the BC designates the class as covering the second and third semesters of college level calculus) These two classes would account for four hours of homework a night if I did it all. I have found that a damage control system works well enough for me to get an A and still tend my responsibilities outside of school. Other things I have going on are a graduation thesis related to hypothermia, an art class, and co-directing several plays for the 5th and 6th grades at my school.

These "non-classes" are by far the most fun I have had in school. The art class is taught by an exceptionally talented man who also understands that "this is a class, and you will learn." It's kind of refreshing. The drama class is both rewarding and wearing. Dealing with 40 energetic kids after lunch is a lot of work, especially in our gym/auditorium at the school. The class is only an hour, but I walk out with a huge sigh of relief every day. However, as tiring as it is, there is something magical about helping kids learn.

With the work I'm doing at home, the homework for my "real" classes, and the time it takes to paint a picture, create a set, and write a thesis, I am stretched for time. With basketball season around the corner and Christmas tree sales knocking on the door, I hope I won't be stretched too thin. Dad has the work of training dogs, and I get the job of taking his responsibilities here at home. I had better stop typing and get back to work on my English paper.

Jim, October 5: I ran an 18 dog team this morning, 11 miles. The dogs are looking good but some of the larger males are losing weight. Astro doesn't eat all I give him and he is looking so skinny. I feel sorry for him but I can't get any meat on his bones.

The weather has finally gotten drier. The sun is out and is a boost to the spirits. The Fall Color is starting to come on vividly.

I have to run the puppy team yet. They are so goofy

during hookup but love to run. I'll take them on a new trail to keep them guessing. Cookie is looking like a natural leader. Hope so.

My best yearling, Becci II is showing signs of a bowel obstruction. I think the silly dog ate rocks and got plugged! I'll have her checked just to be sure. She is worth the cost of surgery.

Rocky, the golden retriever porch-dog is missing again. He is a great buddy. Too bad he's been encouraged to be such an airhead. I can't take time for his testing the limits.

I am finally getting over the headache. I think it was a light case of the flu. I can't afford to stop training just because of the flu.

The weather forecast shows a warming trend. I plan to go home Tuesday and back on Thursday. Chris will come. Good! He is good company. His intelligence and can-do attitude is refreshing.

I'd better go. Otherwise it'll be after dark when I get in.

Jim, October 10: Jennifer and the kids are here with Jennifer's parents, Duane and Peg. The hardwoods are in their best fall colors, a beautiful time for them to be here. This area of Michigan is absolutely stunning when fall colors are out. Rocky, the porch Golden Retriever, who has been lost for over a week, was dropped off last night by the people who found him. They had seen him wandering on the road, and thought he was lost and hungry; he wasn't. The silly dog was happy to get in their truck, and ate a hamburger they offered him. They were deceived! He'll happily get into any truck and eat anything offered. He doesn't seem interested in leaving the porch now.

SledDog Lodge

Jim, October 11: The weather turned windy, cold and wet. The leaves which were so beautiful yesterday were all blowing horizontally today. Wind is howling in the tall pines outside the cabin tonight. It feels like snow is coming. Rocky the porch dog is nervous and wants to come in.

The dogs ran 13 miles today and were visibly ready for more. 18 of them pulled the quad idling in 3rd gear and didn't slow appreciably even after 10 miles. Their conditioning is starting to show. They love running. They love working. They don't ask for thanks, just feed them and let them run. They'll get a big dose of that this year.

We had a squirrel run across the trail about a yard in front the leaders. Boom! Eight of the front dogs were tangled in the brush and the team in an uproar. I am beginning to think the squirrels plan these attacks and then laugh at us from the tree tops.

The spirits of the wilderness were present today. We, the dogs and I, all could feel there were challenges coming we need to prepare for. We know there are places we are going that we've never seen. We know that we'll be tried mightily in ways we've yet to understand. No problem. We'll be ready and we'll deal with it.

Some of us have been there! Peg, Beta, Moe, Bingo, Ketchup, Utah, Alto, have seen the Iditarod, some of them several times. Old Moe knows something big is coming. He, after running 13 miles, came in and growled because somebody peed on his house. After adjusting the smell of his house, he spun dirt to the four winds. Lesser dogs were already sleeping in their houses but not Moe. That old dog is going to make it to Nome this year. I really admire his spirit.

Beta, a living legend, simply gets into harness and pulls the equivalent of four dogs, never slacking. If there were more dogs like him, I'd sure like to have them. Although he has little use for humans, Jennifer has found his sentimental side. They seem to understand each other. It is curious how she is able to connect to the dogs.

More later; I have to sleep before I run dogs in the morning.

Beta Doesn't Understand Cameras

Jim, October 15: A very good day with a rough start and ending! On hookup this morning that silly Brutus nearly ruined the run. He was hooked in lead position. As I was hooking the point dogs, immediately behind leaders, he decided to do his typical burn-outs by throwing lots of dirt behind him A big gob of dirt hit me in the eye and I couldn't do anything more than sit on the ground and dig the dirt out with a finger. Ouch! While I was still sitting, he came up behind me and kissed me behind the ear. What a goofball.

After dinner I decided to run the 10 dog yearling team before dark. While hooking Olive next to Becci, Becci nailed Olive while I still had her in hand. Fortunately, she bit and shook only the harness, missing both my hand and Olive. I don't know what got into her.

When I was half done with hookup, the rain came, cold rain. By the time we finished the 4 mile run, we all were wet. It is so good to be in by the fire. I am reminded why a dry minus 20 degrees is so much better than a wet plus 35.

Jim, October 23: I had 3 rookie leaders in place and decided to take the long way home. They didn't take the Gee command, wanting to go home the short way, so I had to lock the brake on quad and run up to leaders and haul them over to the right trail branch. When running back to the quad they moved back to the wrong way. We repeated 4 times! Finally, noticing leader Brutus back in the team was getting impatient with the nonsense, I exchanged him for one of the rookies. Brutus, no tail wagging, no looking around, head and tail down, looked ominous, like a wet, mad, old Alaskan village dog. His one brown eye and one blue eye looked evil. Certainly he was not a dog to mess with at that point. I got on the quad and gave the command, Ready! Let's Go! Like rockets, the team followed Brutus. The speedometer on the quad went up to 22 MPH until I braked a little. Brutus took the tired team home on a dead run. He got a big hug back at the kennel but didn't like it. Later I gave him a double helping of chow. He liked that and wagged his tail, twice. He is not much of a wiggly, tail wagging, bouncing idiot, but he sure is a hard headed and wonderful sled dog. Wish I had more like him.

Jim, October 25: Sunday morning at SledDog Lodge. Raining! Sometimes wet snow. Penetrating wet; cold! It is real hard to put on the rain gear and go out and run two teams. My warm cup of coffee "is just about my dearest friend." (John Denver's, Sleeping Alone) But this isn't the only time, or the worst, that has to be overcome. The journey to Nome is a lot more than the miles of the race trail.

It is very quiet here, except for the soft raindrops on the metal roof. Have to go!

Jim, October 27: Half inch of snow on ground and snowing lightly. The dog yard is unusually quiet. I'll run a 25 mile camping trip today. We'll go north to the Lake Superior shore about 15 miles and rest there for 2-3 hours and run the 10 miles back home. It is not a far run but it is the first step in getting into the rhythm of run and rest. I think the dogs look forward to a warm bed and dinner when they return.

A somber day! The word I got yesterday was that my mother's condition was deteriorating rapidly. The treatment isn't working and there is no point in escalating aggressive treatment. The phone call could come any minute. But she has enjoyed a long and good life. This is a sad time for the Warren family.

Snow is falling harder. The radar shows it will snow heavily for the next few hours. We'll be running in several inches by the time we return this evening. Next to wind I hate wet snow.

Jim, October 29: A wolf howled just at daybreak. At first I though it was one of the dogs in the dog yard just behind the cabin, but knew it was the wolf when he howled again. Characteristically, the dogs waited a few more seconds before they replied in unison.

After that unforgettable woodland beginning of the day, I harnessed and started a 20 mile run north toward Lake Superior along the West bank of the Little Two Hearted River. Things went wrong when I turned down the wrong trail. We had to make a sharp turn to get back to the race trail. With 18 strong dogs pulling a quad, a sharp turn really puts the dogs at risk, serious risk. The cable gang line can break a leg, neck, crush ribs or cause internal organ damage. Things can get really ugly fast. The dogs sensed we were heading back to the cabin and sped during the turn. Pena got pinned against a large pine tree. To save the dog I gunned the quad ahead. Pena made it but the quad hit the tree; Hard! The front end is all bent up and front wheels are out of alignment. But, Pena was OK. It got worse.

Further down the trail I failed to make the correct turn. Shortly we were trapped into a ½ mile of ORV trail with numerous tight turns with trees. It was pandemonium. Dogs were getting pinched and tangled. I disconnected all neck lines to save the dogs.

Then Carter began screaming. He was dragging upside down with the gangline around both his front legs. All of the dogs were scared. I ran to the front of the team and started disconnecting tug lines to relieve the force on Carter. All the dogs were watching; worried about Carter. Funny, when things get bad the dogs look to me for support and reassurance. They seem to think it'll be alright if I am there. I got Carter loose. He was thankful.

Moments after starting Snowflake got pinched by a tree, then tangled and drug by her rear leg. Again we had panic while I worked, sweating by now, to get her free. We took a short break to settle ourselves and think about best way to get to out of the mess.

I told them I'd get us out just hang with me. We started and leader Brutus went off the trail, I think to straighten out our path to help the team. It didn't help a bit. I thanked him for trying to help but spent a good 15 minutes getting the front-end dogs back on the trail. The trail had gotten so twisty I could only see the last 8-10 dogs. I had to trust Brutus up in front to keep us on trail. We still had ¼ mile to go.

When we finally got to the main trail I was confused as to which way to turn. Brutus refused to take the Gee command. The rookie leader Swen shouldered him in the Gee direction but Brutus nailed him in the ribs. Message: Dogs who want to live don't mess with Brutus. I had to run forward and pull them in the Gee direction. Once moving again, the dogs seemed to forget all about the trauma. They finished the 20 mile run in fine shape. I think they could have gone 30.

Later I got to thinking how much the dogs trust me when things get bad. The worse it is the more they look to me for help and direction. It is very humbling.

Now, downstate at home I think of how different it is here, far away from the soft howl of the timber wolf. It is nice to be with Jennifer and the kids but it is so crowded around here with houses, cars, and lights. I am so thankful for the woods, the dogs, and space. It is freedom.

Jim, November 4: I returned to SledDog Lodge today after having a very bad back for a couple of days from wrestling fire hoses at the fire barn. Weather is wet and rainy with about 3 inches of snow on the ground.

I heard from Sister Lynn who is with other family members at Mom's bedside. Death is near. This is a sad time. Outside the rain is drumming on the metal roof. The wind is whipping the tall pines.

The dogs are definitely ready to take some longer runs. They are ready, the weather is right, and this is the time. Hope the rain is finished by morning.

Jim, November 5: I got the phone call at 5 am that Mom had died. Although this is a sad day, I think it will all work out for the better; she really didn't know where she was. Now she is home with Dad. Time moves on.

We've had high wind with wet snow so I will run with the quad to check the trail. I don't want any surprises like a tree down blocking the trail.

Jim, November 6: Sunny and crisp this morning. The dogs were strong. Eighteen of them pulled the quad in 3rd gear 25 miles. They started at 9-10 MPH and finished at 8-9. Their muscles are starting to strengthen. Their attitudes couldn't be better. They love to pull and run.

Swen is showing signs of an outstanding leader. He is tough, focused, and pays very close attention to the driver. Hartley, his brother, is not far behind but gets easily upset with other dogs and wants to settle the score.... now.

We had a scare today. At about mile 20 we were driving around a small tree and Dell jumped to go around the tree, on the wrong side. Disaster! Before I could get the team stopped by locking all brakes on the quad, there was a loud snap and Dell did a back flip into the pair of dogs behind him. I thought he had broken his neck. I leaped off the quad and when I got to Dell he was checking out the female he'd landed on. Wag, wag, sniff, sniff! Fortunately for him, the brass snap on the neck line broke in two.

I walked out in the dog yard tonight in the full moon. They are content and tired too. Nobody barked, not even Beta. Brutus just watched me and wagged twice when I stopped and looked him in the eye. We speak a lot without using a word.

I remember when he first came to us. He was the guy who played a big role in Cali King's victory in the Junior Iditarod of '02. He looks like an Alaskan village dog and has one blue and one brown eye. With no show of emotion, he is an evil looking dog. He has a look that says, "I am not eating you only because I am not hungry." After a few months he began to warm to us. Now he is my, go-to leader when conditions get ugly. He'd lead the team into Hell if I asked him. I wish I had more like him. His one bad habit is he acts like he is on a joy ride when the snow drifts are deep. When in lead he'll plow right into a 90 degree snow wall then swerve to jump off a 4 foot cliff. The other dogs freak out and get tangled while he is having fun.

Snow! Lots of Snow!

Jim, November 7: 8 AM: Heavy snow just started, wind, visibility about 100 ft, 20 degrees. Three to six inches is forecast with much more tonight. It will be a test of equipment today. The loss of a parent is weighing heavily on my mind today. Not much can be done except work through the grief. Time will heal. Today, the challenge is to get 25 miles on the team. This is a good place to train because it is common to be running into the teeth of a lake-effect storm. But this is nothing compared to the storms that rage on the sea coast between Unalakleet and Nome. There is nothing but sea ice and open water on one side of the trail with tundra on the other side. Wind is fierce, often running 50-60 mph. I hear winds in blow holes can exceed 100 mph, enough to pick up an entire dog team, sled, and driver and actually throw them in a heap, if they are lucky. What little snow falls there is all moving horizontally. Temps can fall to minus 40-50. Horizontal visibility is sometimes 10 feet. Surprisingly vertical visibility is good. Planes can see the mushers on the ground when the mushers can't see their team.

Wow, I was stalling hoping the shower would pass. We now have about 2 inches in about 20 minutes. Maybe I should take the sled instead of the quad. Better get started.

There are twelve inches on the ground and it is 11:30 now, and still coming hard. I'd better get the dogs watered and see if I can find enough stuff under the new snow to get in a run.

Finally we got on the trail at about 2:30 pm with intermittent snow squalls. Dogs were breaking trail all the way with snow nearly to their chest. Brutus was in lead. He ran two co-leaders into the ground so I put Utah up with him. He'd be dead before she got tired. It is funny how some dogs excel. Brutus broke trail in heavy snow for 14 miles before I pulled him back into the team. He didn't want to display pleasure but I could tell he was very happy for the break.

The wind along the forest clear-cuts near Lake Superior was vicious. At times the dogs were barely visible; I could only see shapes moving ahead. The dogs were disappearing into the drifting snow. The snow falling out of the trees would totally block all visibility for a few seconds.

The trail runs about ¼ mile from Lake Superior. The roar of the surf was so load it sounded like hundreds of big aircraft jet engines. To bad there isn't some way to harness some of the energy of the surf.

It is uncanny how the dogs remember a trail. Utah, in lead, tried to turn the team onto a side trail that had not been used since last January, and used only once, during the Tahquamenon Race. There was no visible trail! No vehicle tracks at all and ferns looked just like the rest of the woods. I knew it was the trail only because of a faint red dot on a tree. She remembered the trail she used almost a year ago, and it was buried under 3 feet of snow then. How can they have such precise memory? Dogs are amazing creatures.

I thought the dogs would be dead tired when they finished the 25 mile run. Surprise! Tired yes, but still had plenty of energy. Their stamina is really developing well this year. Good, they are going to need it!

I am very tired. It is 8:30 and I'm going to hit the sack.

Jim, November 8: A good run today. The dogs are getting very conditioned. It is wonderful to see them growing in power and stamina. They came in today and were ready for chow and a short rest. The meat wasn't yet thawed so I had to delay feeding. They complained about the delay.

I've been watching a National Geographic Explorer show on TV about climbing Denali. What a grand mountain. Seeing it once is a thrill of a lifetime. I am reminded the Iditarod Trail crosses the Alaska Range not too far from Denali. Fortunately we'll cross at Rainy Pass around 3000 feet in elevation. That is high enough. There are no trees in the pass and the wind can and does blow. With a little luck we'll get through there in the daylight. Then ahead is the Dalzell Gorge. It has the reputation of a very difficult stretch of trail and best traveled in daylight. You spend 2 days climbing to the pass then spend two hours going back down. The trail winds, sometimes steeply, down a canyon crossing the river several times. There are many drop-offs, ice bridges, and sharp turns. My plan is to pull many of the tug lines off the dogs so they can't rocket us down hill like idiots. Getting into Rohn in good shape will be a very happy occasion.

Jim, November 9: Sunday morning; temp is 9 degrees;

sun is rising. Nice. We'll run about 30 miles today. I hope things go smoothly.

I noticed a bunch of coyote tracks in the yard. They ran all over but didn't go near the dogs. Nor did they stop to eat the meat scraps made by chopping with ax the frozen 50 pound blocks of meat. What were they up to?

Tomorrow will be busy. I will run 35 miles then clean up to go home for a day visit. They scheduled a memorial service for Mom. I guess I must attend, but it seems rather difficult with all that needs to be done here. OK; I'll attend! But we will be out of luck for running dogs for the first week of deer season. The hours of legally using the quad is limited during daylight. If I want to run at all it will be at night. OK, I can do that too.

Jim, November 11: I attended a memorial service for Mom today in Midland. Then I drove back to the UP to feed dogs and get ready to run next day. It was not a good trip. The 300 mile trip was much too far to drive alone already feeling depressed. Almost there, in the dark and falling snow, I missed the turn from I-75 to M-123 and ended up in Sault Ste Marie. It took me another hour but finally made it and fed dogs. They always cheer me; things are looking up now. An old trick learned long ago is simply called 'a water glass full of scotch'. I learned from a crusty old fireman how to deal with post traumatic stress. This brain numbing technique works. No more needs to be said. Tomorrow will be here soon.

Jim, November 12: Big storm forecast for tonight: Five to 10 inches with 30-45 MPH winds with another 5 inches tomorrow morning. So I got a bunch of stuff done here in prep for an early winter. Then I took the quad out and checked out a 45 mile trail I'll run next.

Wow! I went outside on the porch to check the weather and noticed a pair of yellow eyes looking at me at the edge of the woods. When he turned slowly to leave, it looked like the wolf but can't be sure unless I go out and check the tracks. I'd like to but just don't have the guts, even armed. It is a windy, spooky night. I think I'll crawl in the sack and listen to the wind and snow hitting the roof.

Jim, November 13: A lot of wind last night but only a little snow. Good! Forecast is for 1-3 inches more of lake effect snow with winds at 30 gusting to 55 miles per hour. This will be good training for tundra conditions.

The last time I was in Unalakleet for two days winds were 40-50 gusting 70-80 MPH. It is hard to describe winds like that. When on the trail about all you can do is to pray winds are from behind and not in your face. I talked to a guy who had a side wind blowing him across glare ice toward the open water. The wind had flipped the sled and knocked many of the dogs down. He was finally able to stop the slide by jamming the sled's snow hook into the ice. He was very happy to get back on good traction.

Today we will try to do a 40 mile run in a different location to keep the dogs guessing. We'll head for the Whitefish Point area. Hope the snow squalls are not too bad. This should be a good day for training for adverse conditions.

Last night the wind had the trees bending way over. There are a number of tall pines near the cabin that were really bent over. Strange they don't snap.

I wonder where my wolf-like visitor is this morning. The dogs got pretty excited last night but it was probably just the wind. I'll count dogs just to be sure one isn't missing.

Chris November 16: Well, things have settled into a pretty solid routine here at home. I am even able to get everything done. Except for that pesky English homework, that doesn't ever seem to get done. I also seem to have some amount of free time. I even found time to go deer hunting yesterday. I shot a deer, but to my disappointment not fatally. However, not even that could dampen my spirits. Spending an entire day sitting and doing nothing of value for anyone but myself was really relaxing. I'm still in a good mood. Unfortunately, I doubt that I will be able to hunt the rest of this deer season. Dad is leaving tomorrow for SledDog Lodge, along with the temporary relief from chores.

Jim, November 19: Just as I got 18 dogs hooked up this morning I noticed both leaders had disappeared. The dogs behind the leaders had chewed off their tug lines and they had left and were somewhere rocketing down the trail. I had to quickly unhook the 16 remaining dogs and head out with the quad hoping to find them. I was able to track them in the sand. Ten miles out I found them blocked by a fallen tree across the trail. What a relief.

Later I thought about the sight of 2 experienced Iditarod dogs standing in the trail with a big pine tree fallen across the trail in front of them. They easily could have run around either end of the tree... the forest floor was quite open and free of brush. But they just didn't think outside of the box. Is there a message here for humans? I think so.

Jim, November 24: I finished running 160 miles over the last 3 days. Snow, rain, lots of rain, finally today snow, cold and blowing. Tough weather! Dogs came in covered with ice from the puddles that splashed and froze on their coats. They were clinking when they ran. The tug lines became like a stick, no longer a rope.

Most of the dogs are rising to the occasion. Tough weather, tough trails, bad weather, and repeated runs even when tired is all part of training. They are muscling out and are starting to look like Arnold S. They pulled the quad a solid 40 miles today at speeds from 8 to 10 MPH. They will need all the conditioning they can get.

Leaders are an important part of the mix. A musher who has seen many miles behind the dogs is an asset too. An example of the learning came tonight 5 miles from camp. The temp was dropping through 20 and, surprise, the dogs started treating puddles like they were instant death. On a turn in the dark where I couldn't see the leaders and most of the team, the leaders apparently dodged around a puddle creating some slack in the line. My guess is Dell jumped on the wrong side of a tree causing a tangle. By the time I got there I had 18 dogs jumping in a ball trying to get out of the freezing puddle. Even worse, the ½ inch of ice on all the snaps made it impossible to release the dogs. Wow! So I jumped into the puddle which was over my boots and started pulling the dogs out of the trees one at a time. But putting them in the puddle wasn't working because they just jumped back into the tangle. Sitting down and crying wasn't likely to help either. Finally I managed to find Dell under the pile of dogs with his head wedged behind the tree. I was able to squeeze him back far enough to free him. On command the whole ball of dogs started to move ahead. They slowly pulled the quad through the puddle while I sloshed alongside with water to my knees and over my boots. What a sight; a ball of tangled dogs pulling a quad out of a freezing puddle in a snow storm in the dark. My state of mind improved quickly once out of the puddle.

Fortunately, my feet only had a few miles of cold to endure before we got to the dog yard. But then it took another hour to unhook and feed the team.

Jim, November 25: Time to go back downstate for Thanksgiving, and Rocky the Golden Retriever porch dog is missing again. I was keeping him tied to the porch, but must have forgotten when I went to Shaw's to pick up dog meat. Daughter Whitney will not be happy.

Jim, November 30: The following entry contains graphic descriptions of a highway accident scene. You may wish to skip it.

I got up just as dawn was breaking. I was reeling from a bad dream, a very bad dream. My head felt swollen. But I had to run dogs today. As the gas lamp began shedding light on the kitchen counter I noticed a water glass with liquid in the bottom from melted ice cubes. The liquid was slightly colored from the scotch whiskey that had filled it the night before. My eyes moved to the still damp shirt hanging over the wood heater. It had a partially washed out blood stain on the sleeve. It wasn't a dream! It had been real.

Driving back to SledDog Lodge had taken much longer because of the slippery roads and the snow storm. I saw a flash of light ahead on the highway, then momentarily headlights aiming my direction in my lane. As I got closer it was obviously an accident. As a volunteer firefighter I was in the habit of carrying my turnout gear and a medical bag. My years in a rural fire department had prepared me for what I was about to face. I positioned my truck on the highway to protect the injured and aimed the headlights to light the accident scene. I grabbed my medical bag from the back seat and ran up to the crushed vehicles to assess the situation. It was bad. I asked a female motorist who had stopped to call 911 and report an accident with injuries and a firefighter on scene.

My quick assessment was grim. I found 1K, (killed), 1 terminally injured but conscious, 2 injured and bleeding heavily with death likely without immediate care, and one young mother apparently uninjured but looking for her child. I asked the female motorist to call again and tell the 911 dispatcher to send everything they can get... we have several severely injured...more info will be coming. Moments later I asked her to call 911 again and tell them we have a ruptured gas tank with fuel all over the scene.

This was a triage situation. You train for this but hope you never have to make these decisions. But there was no time to waste. I asked the young mother to get in the face of the terminally injured person and keep her talking. She asked, "Will Mom be alright?" She answered herself, "She isn't going to be alright." I replied, "Just keep her talking the best you can." I placed the hand of the injured Mom in hand of the young mother hoping to provide a little comfort for her last minutes.

As I ran to one of the bleeding patients, I notice an old firefighter hurrying onto the scene. He was pulling on his turn-out coat. He wore thick glasses and a short salt and pepper beard. His hair was mostly white giving a clue to his advancing age. He looked worried. I yelled, "1K, 1 terminal and two serious bleeders. Take that bleeder over there." The Young Mother talking to the terminally injured Mom murmured, "Oh my God!"

To my dismay the old firefighter was standing still, not moving. He stammered, "I'm not good at medical. I'm not even licensed." I replied, "That's OK! You will be working under my medical license. You can be in charge of the scene and I'll be in charge of medical. Right now, that patient over there is yours!"

I ran to the other bleeding patient. I placed pressure to stop the flow of precious blood while trying to do further assessment. She looked ok except for the ugly gash. Her gray color and clammy feeling skin was ominous signs of shock. I prayed for the fast arrival of the ambulances to get an IV started. Time was running out for this person. But the pressure was stopping the blood flow. There was hope.

At that moment the old firemen yelled for me. I motioned for a bystander to come over and instructed her on how to hold pressure. Her hands shaking, she applied pressure as I had instructed but just then the patient moaned. She pulled back, then gasped as the blood began spurting when the pressure was removed. She reapplied pressure. I went to aid the old fireman. The smell of gasoline was very strong. We were kneeling in a puddle. We were in grave risk but kept working anyway. Snow was falling very heavily giving the scene an eerie look in the headlights and flashing red strobe of my truck.

The young mother who was to keep the terminal Mom talking started to scream, "She is not breathing." The old fireman started in that direction but I grabbed his arm and said quietly, "There was nothing we could do."

His patient was in an awkward position which wouldn't allow the pressure point to be accessed. We had to move the person. Working in the dark and without enough help we carefully but quickly moved the person to the snowy roadway. It worked; the bleeding was controlled.

It seemed to take forever but finally there were a number of local EMS personal on scene. We found the lifeless body of the child that had been thrown from the vehicle on impact, hidden under the snow. It was a difficult time for even the most hardened care givers.

There was no need for me to stay. I worked my way over to my truck somewhat in shock and exhausted. As I sat in my truck looking for a convenient path to leave the now congested accident scene I noticed the old fireman sit down on the bumper of the fire truck and slowly slump forward, his head low.

With knowing eyes I watched for a few seconds as he began sobbing. I knew what he was feeling. I was not much better off. I desperately wanted to put time and distance between me and this accident scene. But I couldn't let him sit there alone.

As I walked over to him my bright musher headlamp illuminated him like an actor on a stage. He was sitting with his elbows on his knees and his head in his hands. His soot stained turnout gear was evidence of a veteran firefighter. The knees of his bunker pants had fresh blood stains. He reeked of the gasoline we both had been kneeling in.

He hadn't noticed my approach until I put my hand on his shoulder. Startled, he looked up directly into the bright beam of my headlamp. His face will stick in my mind forever. Wet snow and tears were freezing in the mostly white beard. His face and glasses were speckled with blood. A half hour earlier he stood between life and eternity for a person he never knew, on a dark, windy, snow covered highway, in a blizzard. Now, he was a broken soul with nobody but a stranger to comfort him. I sat with him; we talked. I couldn't rid my mind of the hundreds of firefighters who lost their lives running up smoke filled stairwells of the World Trade Center.

On the remaining drive to SledDog Lodge, I began wondering. Where did that old firefighter come from? Was he, like me, just a passerby who was at the right spot during a family's darkest hour? Do you believe in angels?

I'll never know. Nor will I ever know the name of the 'Old Fireman' or the name of the family. But his face will stick in my mind forever. But, I am glad I could help. Yes, I am glad I could help even though the emotional load was almost unbearable.

But today I have to run dogs. We must be ready for Iditarod in a few weeks. I am again reminded, there is a lot more to Iditarod than the miles of the race trail.

Jim, December 5: Well here I am at 30,000 feet above Minnesota enroute to Anchorage to the Iditarod Rookie meeting. I am not sure why the meeting takes two full days but will know more soon. I presume they want to be sure we know what we are getting into. Well, too late! I do! Training has been grueling and long. Dogs are getting conditioned. I hope I am too although sometimes I think 'rundown' would better describe my condition.

Looking down now on some of the snow covered mountains below I am reminded I'll be running a team of world class dogs somewhere down there. It looks daunting even from here. Eleven hundred miles is a VERY long way.

We have a lot more training to do. The dogs have about 600 miles on them now and I am aiming for 1500 to 1800 before I am confident we are ready. Only the toughest will make that level of mileage without failing. Only the strong, and probably dumb, will get the chance. Wonder if they think that about the driver?

I have been thinking about how nice it was to be home last night instead of alone at SledDog Lodge. Chris has become a very capable young man. He has been handling the tree sales like a pro. Whitney is hammering away at her new school. She is growing into a solid and capable woman. They grow so fast. When they are gone, I think adjusting to their absence will be one of the hardest things I have faced. I hope Jennifer is there so we can make the adjustment together.

In the meantime I am solely focused on one goal. Arriving with my dog team in Nome! Until we arrive, or it is impossible to continue, I will focus my sweat, my heart and my soul on the goal.

The dogs, especially the experienced Iditarod dogs, know. They watch my every move with incredible understanding. They speak too, not with words, but with a range of looks and body language. We understand each other more than can be explained.

I have my favorites! Brutus is incredible when in a pinch. His choppy gait may limit his ability to go the distance. Some of the dogs move so fluidly they seem to float. But Brutus got hot and tired Weds. He decided he'd take the team down the middle of the busy county road where it was a little easier running. I can't blame him but it is too risky. While he was in lead there was no way he'd take the team on the right side, Gee Over command. So, I stopped the team to move him out of lead. He knew immediately why we had stopped. He turned around and placed himself along side of a cute female. Of course I yelled at him and dragged him forward. But I relented and placed him where he wanted to go. Brutus, you owe me one now.

Jim and Brutus

Penya is a surprising tough little leader. In summer she gets a little pudgy and takes a while to run it off. But, I can run her a hundred miles in lead. She finally will start lying down when we stop and put her chin on her front feet, tired. When I get back on to go she doesn't even look back at me. She just cocks one ear toward me and waits for the command to go. Instantly she is on her feet and we are off. Tough!

Then there are a bunch of dogs that just pull and pull. They are the ones who never get any attention mostly because they do just what they are supposed to. They might be the real heroes and we don't seem to recognize them for what they contribute. They are Ruby, Stormy, Hartley, Faith, Moe, and Beta, just to name a few.

Utah

Utah is unbeatable. Tough, smart, fast and doesn't tire. However, she is a real hell raiser with other females. She starts and always loses fights. One night last year on a snowy run all the females in the team jumped her and I couldn't stop them. I thought they'd kill her. I finally won. Standing in a circle of blood stained snow I checked out Utah who surprisingly didn't have too many big holes in her. She pulled the final 10 miles back home, bleeding. She couldn't get up to get out of her box in the morning. I carried her outside so she could pee. By evening she ate out of my hand and was able to walk. I gave her a few days off. She has settled down a little but still I watch her closely.

Then there are the boneheads. Pokey just can't run on his own side when alongside a female. I guess he wants to cuddle on the run. I can't let that inefficiency hinder the team. Every step, every breath, everything has to be efficient and focused on getting there. Nome.

Jim, December 8: After 2 days of Alaska, I am refreshed. Sleeping on a floor in a sleeping bag has become a way of life. So has sleeping on the ground in rain, snow, or alongside the team. Isn't retirement supposed to be sitting in front of a fireplace with your feet on a golden retriever while reading a book and sipping an adult beverage? I wonder if I'll live long enough to do that. Probably not!

Anyway, we were spoken to by the best of the best. Jeff King had several words of wisdom. One statement he made still rings in my ears. He said, "If you aren't at least a little bit scared, you are crazy." We spent one day at Martin Buser's. What a class act and outstanding person. I learned a lot.

While doing this Jen, Chris and Whitney have been doing a marvelous job at keeping the tree sales moving very well. I am so impressed with their ability to work together and get things done. I owe them a lot for all their hard work.

We are coming into the Minneapolis Airport and I'll be home by 10 pm. It will be nice to be home.

Jim, December 12: Back at SledDog Lodge. I stayed at home for an additional day because of weather and the opportunity to visit with Jennifer's parents Duane and Margaret who were helping with Christmas trees. It was a nice visit. But when I turned in the driveway here I got stuck in the 1.5 feet of snow. So, with darkness falling, I backed out the quad from the trailer and ferried 12 dogs and all the gear to the cabin. I finished at 9:30, tired. I woke at 6:30 and got things moving. I need to get the sled loaded and ready for the 300 mile Seney 300. I don't need to run this but is a good chance to practice my distance skills. The discipline in caring for the dogs is vital to saving time which translates directly into better rest for dogs and me.

Snow is still falling, windy and 10 degrees. I had planned on running the dogs about 20 miles for exercise but may not be able to since I have no way to break trail. The snow was too deep for the quad and I didn't bring the snowmobile. Maybe if I waited a snowmobile would run down the trail to break trail for us and then we could run. It didn't happen.

I am looking forward in a big way to next weekend when Whitney will be here with me. She is good company! She has grown up so much in the last few months. This is good but is a reminder that soon she will be moving on. That will be a sad day but I will be an encouraging Dad, even with a breaking heart.

I remember last summer when she helped me for most of a week revamping the plumbing in the cabin. She was so good and learned so fast I think she could probably do the next plumbing job herself. That was a wonderful week.

I sure hope something doesn't come up that causes her to change her mind about coming next week.

Time to water dogs and get the sled inside to start packing. This will be a pre-Iditarod shakedown.

Chris, December 15: Lying in bed this morning at 5:30 I was having an awful time. Already having slept through the alarm for half an hour, I couldn't move. The last two weeks have been absolutely brutal. Working the Christmas Tree Farm as owner and operator has me literally beat. In addition to the normal duties of a manager, I have been working the sales lot as well. It is physically demanding work, to say the least. According to my sister Whitney, I was "burning the candle at both ends before", but with the tree sales, I've "started a fire in the middle too." I have found my limit. Months of late nights, and now two weeks of minimal sleep and manual labor have me on the ropes. I just want this month to end. It's only a week before sales end, only a week.

Jim, December 18: Just left the Seney 300 Musher Banquet here in Grand Marais, MI and am in the motel room getting ready for bed. It occurred to me it has been about a week since I slept in a bed, or without my hat on. Yes, sleeping in a bed is going to feel strange. Some of the time on the trail I slept on straw along side of the dogs.

Tonight the North wind is about 40 mph coming across Lake Superior with snow, very cold and damp. I almost wish I was back on the trail, dressed for the weather.

Just before the Musher Banquet Veterinarian, Dr Tom Gustafson came over to the motel room to work on Ruby, the tough little female we got from Jeff King. She had a slash on her front leg that needed suturing. We sedated her then placed her on the table in the motel room and worked for a good half hour to get the wound repaired. She will be fine.

Well the Seney was a case of good and bad. Although I didn't need to run it for an Iditarod qualifier, I chose to run it to fine tune some of the processes, like sled packing, checkpoint discipline, dog feeding, and musher feeding. I want the actual running of Iditarod to be somewhat boring to save time for other learning.

The first trail leg starting at Grand Marais, a little less than 50 miles, was fun. Dogs were very strong so I braked heavily the first hour, then braked steady for the second hour, and finally intermittently for the balance of the run. The run was about 5 hours.

After a 7 hour rest at Sunken Lake Gravel Pit they were

excited to leave the checkpoint and didn't even let me wait my turn. With me standing on the snow hook, they pulled it loose and we were off on the exit trail from the checkpoint. The sled hit a large steel chain under the snow and flipped me violently. I jerked the sled upright and 50 feet further a repeat but without an excuse that time. I was mad! "Ok, you guys want to run, go for it, but you'll be tired at the next checkpoint and it will serve you right." So they ran hard with no stops for about 35 miles. By then a couple of teams had passed me including Wendy with Lloyd Gilbertson's Stage dogs, but nobody else was close. Then Kate started limping and spinning her tail, a clear sign she was in distress so I slowed to see if she could hang on until the checkpoint. She made it but was extremely tired. I found she had a sore shoulder muscle so decided to drop her from the remainder of the race.

To my surprise they were not tired leaving the Haverstock Creek checkpoint 6 hours later. They were really fired up. A tight twisty trail section seemed to light them up even more. Pepsi an older leader freaked out when he saw liquid on an ice covered puddle. He balked so hard he backed into Hartley in the third row of dogs. No dog puts his butt in Hartley's face and gets away with it. Dog fight! Swen instantly joined. Utah never misses a good fight. Even Alto was laying a few bites on any dog that came up for air. But I got it stopped before the fun got too far out of hand. I pulled Pepsi back into the team and made sure I had solid leaders in front because there was a serious steam crossing coming up. Now they seemed even more fired up. The sled was ricocheting off trees. We passed a team at about twice their speed, flipped once but righted instantly and hardly missed a beat. Then ... a leaning tree at the apex of a turn was about to rip the handle bar off the sled I stepped out to wrench the sled over. This is at about 15 mph mind you. I slipped and felt a tear in my right thigh going all the way to my lower back. This time with the sled on its side I barely could right it. My right leg was nearly unusable. This would play a bigger role later.

Nearing the stream crossing, still running like idiots, we brushed against a large tree causing the sled bag to open loosing my extra trail clothing. I dropped the snow hook and instead of coming to a reasonable stop we stopped instantly causing me to slam against the back of the sled. I looked back at the lost bag of clothing 50 yards behind, then looked ahead at the animated barking and jumping team and knew I could not risk losing the team to try and retrieve the lost item. So I tried to pull the snow hook but it wouldn't budge. It had buried itself in a tree root and I couldn't budge it with the dogs pulling hard against the rope. After several tries, it suddenly broke free and the dogs leaped forward with even more vigor. The good news is we broke around a turn just before the water crossing and the leaders were into the stream before they could think. They charged across to my delight.

Later at the Hardman checkpoint my injured leg cramped. After 10 minutes of jumping around in the very dark bunkhouse angering very tired mushers, some of whom were sleeping on the floor, I grabbed my parka and boots and jumped around outside on the fresh snow in my bare feet for another 10 minutes. The cramp persisted. I couldn't get my boots on so I had to go in the cabin. After an hour the cramp subsided but it had become clear to me that I couldn't drive the team, especially that team, with one leg. Unhappy, still hoping for a miracle cure, I resigned my self to giving the dogs a "24 hour" at the checkpoint and trying to run back to Grand Marais when the teams returned.

After the 24 hour and still feeling a lot of pain, Ben Stamm agreed to run the dogs back to Grand Marais. It was not a happy moment to see my dogs leave the checkpoint and me not with them. But Ben had fun.

The Seney 300

Jim, December 23: Whitney and I arrived back at SledDog Lodge with all 37 dogs. Chris and Jennifer will arrive Christmas Eve and stay until after New Years. I couldn't be happier to have these guys here. There has been too much time alone here this fall.

My leg injury is worse than I first thought. It is a torn hamstring and will take weeks to heal completely. With my crippled left foot, I really need a healthy right leg to do serious sled driving. I am working with a sport physical therapist to hasten the return to normal. In the meantime I am having a tough time tending dogs in the dog yard with the 2 feet of snow. I now have more empathy for the dogs when they get a pulled muscle.

Jim, December 25: Christmas morning at SledDog Lodge couldn't be any nicer. I am up alone, 6am, sitting by the fire with a cup of coffee and am happy! It occurred to me I've been retired for almost 3 years and haven't yet slept-in. Sleeping-in to me is getting up AFTER daybreak. It has nothing to do with a clock. I just start thinking of what I want to get done that day and just can't wait to get at it. Why change now!

It also occurred to me we don't have a family Christmas tree! After spending our time growing and selling thousands, we don't even have one. Maybe it is because we are a driven and focused family. Jennifer is working hard as a corporate attorney. Chris is finishing HS, second in his class, graduating early to be able to go to Alaska and see Iditarod. Whitney is working equally hard to get her first year of HS math and science in the A category. Then, they all worked a lot of extra hours on tree sales during December while I was in Alaska for Iditarod rookie meeting, and then running the Seney 300. Maybe there just wasn't any time for our own family Christmas tree. We'll make up for it this week with our dogs.

It is at times like this when I understand how fortunate and blessed I am. Although sick with the flu, Jennifer tried to get us to attend a church service in Newberry on Christmas Eve. She is the spiritual leader of the family, followed closely by Whitney, and keeps us directed with the right priorities. This family is very fortunate to have her.

Whitney is up and has asked to have a, "Mr. Hardman breakfast." She remembers eating at Al's cabin once and made a mental note of what is a great breakfast. This is going to be tough order to fill but I am going to give it a shot.

Jim, December 26: Before dawn again if you haven't guessed. Yesterday was a wonderful day. I sure like having my family here. I couldn't be happier. Earlier this morning while lying in my bunk practicing sleeping-in I got to thinking how important holidays are. They got started in prehistoric times and probably have a value as an aid to mental health. I used to think of them as an unfortunate interruption of things that need to get done. Silly me!

Chris and Whit ran 8 dog teams yesterday. The dogs were fast and strong. About 10 miles out we encountered a 3 mile section that contained a succession of steep but short hills. I stopped my snowmobile several times expecting the teams to slow somewhat on the uphill sections. To my surprise the teams appeared almost instantly still running as they crested the hills. The dogs were running the uphill like they were not even there. This is good; they need this level of conditioning.

Jennifer although sick with the flu put her mark on the organization of the cabin. It looks better now. She may be sicker than she thinks but she keeps going anyway. Because of a severe bout with meningitis a few years ago she lost the ability to run a fever so she sometimes doesn't know when she is really sick. Hope she feels better today.

I am taking the snowmobile this morning and checking a 50 mile loop that will take us across the Wide-waters of the Betsy River. I have to check the ice to be sure we can run on the trails I scouted last summer. It will be a good loop if OK. I think it can become one leg of a 200 mile training loop. We have a good place to drop our supplies for the wilderness camps. The training loop will include the Wide-waters Loop, the Rohn Outpost west of Grand Marais, and Al Hardman's cabin North of McMillan.

Chris and Whit will run the puppies today.

Jim, December 29: Another early morning for me at SledDog Lodge. Jen, Chris, and Whit are sleeping. Weather is still too warm; the snow is soft and dogs would sink to their chest so we'll wait until tomorrow to make a run toward Rohn outpost near Grand Marais. Today we'll do dog chores like clip toenails and check collar tightness. I also need to check harness sizes; their size changes during training.

The reason for getting up early is to do final Iditarod calendar planning such as getting together my weekly to-do list. All supplies need to be ordered NOW. Drop bags, about 2000 pounds, are to be delivered to Ludington, MI, on 4 Feb for shipment to Alaska. This is a big effort with completeness essential to our success.

Fortunately I have a very detailed Microsoft Excel spreadsheet from Al Hardman that details by checkpoint every item essential to the trip. This tool has made planning much simpler and is added insurance against overlooking something important. All I had to do was adjust the spreadsheet to include my preferences. During the race I will carry a printout of this spread sheet so I will be able to know exactly what supplies will be waiting at which checkpoint.

Jennifer is still sick with the flu. She still keeps going, somehow. She always amazes me with how she finds ways to keep going even if it is for a few minutes at a time.

With about 1000 miles already on the dogs the plan is to keep piling up the miles with a target of 1800. The runs will be no shorter than 40-50 miles with many of them back-to-back runs with overall trips of 150-200 miles. The more we can do run-rest training the better for both dogs and drivers. This will make Jan and Feb pretty intense months.

Chris graduates from High School on January 22nd. In 3 ½ years he not only finished HS with excellent grades in all the tough AP math and science but also has tested out of a bunch of 1st year college classes. Amazing! He is an excellent student. He has colleges falling over one another trying to get him. I hope he continues to put all his intellectual horsepower to use for himself. It is up to him from here. On second thought, it has been up to him for some time already. I am happy for him and pleased to have him as a son.

Jim, December 31: New Years Eve morning is just one more day to run dogs. We prepared for this run yesterday so we can get off early this morning. We are running a 50 mile loop west to the Two Hearted River. Chris and Whit will run 8 dog teams and I'll run ahead to warn oncoming snowmobilers. Some snow has fallen and the wind is raking the tall pines but the temperature is still hanging in the low 30s; too warm.

Chris checked out Swen, one of our powerhouse two-year-olds, and found a major knot in the muscle of his rear leg. Chris massaged him for quite some time. Swen fell asleep in his arms. The dogs really appreciate when we are working trying to help them.

We were up late building neck and tug lines. It goes a lot faster when everybody joins in. Evenings here with the family has been a real boost to me. Usually, after a day with dogs I am so tired I fall asleep as soon as I sit down. Once I woke about midnight still sitting in the big chair. I can't risk sitting down when I have something cooking or the generator is running.

Jim, January 2: The dog yard will be different this

evening. Gone will be the three head lamps and the chatter coming from happy dogs and people. It was a good holiday but is sadly coming to an end. I enjoyed their company as did the dogs. We, the dogs and I, will carry on.

But right now I'd better get the bacon and pancakes cooking so this gang can stumble to life. The smell of breakfast is irresistible to teenagers. Am I bad or what?

Jim, January 5: I returned from a 110 mile training run in two legs in a little over 24 hours. The dogs are physically well conditioned but need some mental toughness. The 7 team dogs never had a slack tug. The 5 leaders tired in lead. I had to rotate them to keep us moving, especially when breaking trail. Managing a dog team is tricky. I have a lot to learn.

I left here about 3:30 pm traveling the trails along Lake Superior heading for Rohn outpost West of Grand Marais, about 47 miles. The wind was strong out of the Northwest with a dropping temperature, snow squalls were almost certain. No kidding! On the trail section just above the beach the wind was ferocious. The snow was so heavy I had to turn off the headlamp and run in the dark. As we approached the lake the roar of the surf in the dark scared the dogs so much the leaders stopped. I had to run up and lead them for a few yards to convince them the roar wasn't going to kill us. I wasn't so sure. It was ominous. While traveling along the shore in the dark you could see the big breakers tearing at the shore. It makes you feel very small, out in the dark, with the heavy snow stinging your face. The wind was brutal. I was cold, real cold.

The dogs were outstanding. Siesta kept a steady 12 mph pace up and down the hills. We stopped twice for doggie snacks and for a couple of tangles. We met some snowmobilers who were singing... very drunk. When they saw the reflecting dog eyes, the flashing red strobe on the leaders, and all the reflective harnesses, they yelled, "It is Santa Claus and his 12 hound dogs." We weren't amused.

Then on the snowmobile trail 7 miles from a plowed road we met a car, stuck. The person was from Georgia and had driven 30 miles from Munising on the snowmobile trail with his car! His wife was not impressed at all. I gave them my cell phone to call 911 for assist. I hope they made it out OK.

We arrived at Rohn (the U.P. version) in about 5 hours for an average speed of 10 MPH. Good! I bedded and fed the dogs, then waited for Al Hardman, Jim Conner, and Al's Handler Gregg Hickmann who were expected to arrive later. It was a good run.

I haven't said much to anyone about the problem with the pulled hamstring injury I suffered in the Seney 300. This was my first time on the sled since the injury. I was paranoid about re-injury. The doc says the chance of re-injury in an activity like mushing is very high and it will take months to completely heal. A re-injury would put Iditarod in serous jeopardy. So I have lain awake at night forcing myself to think through a fall-back plan, just in case. We have said all along the Iditarod plan was a 3 year window with intention to run 2 out of the 3. Fall back would be to run UP 200 since it has easy trails, maybe run Race to the Sky in Montana, but head to Alaska to handle for someone to ensure we learn all we can in preparation for the next year. But, the target is and will remain a healthy dog team finishing in Nome.

The leg occasionally causes me to limp and when I need power it is weak. It aches at night but not so much that an Advil doesn't take care of it. When I carry buckets of dog food I really notice the weakness. For now I'll do what I can to get stronger and follow the therapist's instructions. A challenge I didn't anticipate was getting this aging frame to the Nome finish line.

Jim, January 6: I checked the dog training log and found I am behind on dog training miles with no time to recover. I am in danger of having to scuttle the plans for Iditarod. My only hope is that Chris follows through on coming to train with me for the last few weeks. I need to confirm his intentions.

e-Mail: Hi Chris. RE: Your Role in Iditarod Preparation

I just revised my projection for dog training miles for Iditarod. I think I can get about 1400 miles compared to a target of 1800 miles. The shortfall was caused by Mom's funeral, Rookie Meeting in Alaska, and my leg injury in Seney 300. Here are my thoughts on how to proceed.

I am hesitant to try to run Iditarod if miles are below what would be a reasonable level. I will find out what is a reasonable cutoff from Al Hardman.

I will focus on the 20-22 dogs that have the highest chance of making the final cut for Iditarod,

I will organize setting up the drop bags so that time is as short as possible.

Lake effect snow is starting today and will cut the miles by half because of the time spent opening trail. The alternative is running down the plowed roads but that sets up the dogs for wrist injury so that should not become an excessively used alternative. I'll have to team up with Ed Stielstra and Gregg Hickmann for trail breaking.

Your role in this is critical and likely will make the difference in having adequate preparation to allow us to go. Key tasks are running snowmobile to break trail, running second team, and errands like picking up dog food, or delivering drop bags to Ludington. Also, sharing dog care chores will allow more time for better care and healthier dogs.

Please call me and let me know what you are willing to do? You talked as if you were going to focus on dogs after graduation on Jan 22. If that is true, my anxiety level drops a lot because it again looks like there is a chance.

As always, I have a fall back plan. Even with OK preparation, if something should happen like I re-injure my leg, I would want at least one of us to run the UP 200 with its easy trails. Then we could go to Iditarod as handler for Al or somebody else, or just do a lot of spectating.

So, as you can see, I am a little overwhelmed by the tasks to be done in the next few days. Your help will be greatly appreciated but you are free to make the decision and I'll adjust accordingly

Please let me know your thoughts. Jim Warren

Jim, January 7: SledDog Lodge: Al and Gregg ran the 60 miles to here. I was planning to run back with them returning today. But, I had decided against running two 60 plus runs back to back and instead planned to run with a group of dogs coming off medical time-off. Good thing. Just after Al left, a water pipe burst. All of yesterday was spent fixing the piping. Temperature was hanging at about -8 for much of the day.

Today; I will do what I planned to do yesterday. As soon as daylight arrives I'll water dogs and get the harnesses out and gangline connected. If I can get off before 10 am I can run a longer run or come in early and take out another team. There is an additional 10 inches of lake effect snow on top of the 7 inches of yesterday, so we'll be breaking trail for much of the run. This is good training for the dogs; not

fun, but good mental conditioning. They'd rather run fast
with easy pulling. They will be happy with the temp which
is about zero with brisk winds.

Brutus, finally, seems to have healed from his puncture
wound of his wrist. He is behind on conditioning miles so
he'll get a big dose of runs to try to help him catch up. He is
an outstanding leader and would be a big loss. Kate seems
to have overcome her pulled muscle. She is so happy to be
back running. Swen is still ailing from his muscle tear. I'll
have the vet look at him this week. He is a phenomenal
dog. I hate to lose him for the season. Raheim has a serious
ding; he can hardly run. But I cannot find the problem. He
refuses to yelp or pull back when palpated. I'll have him
examined by the vet too.

On a positive note, Chris confirmed his intent to dive
into dogs upon his early graduation from High School. This
is a major cushion to be sure we have proper dog training.
Things like a burst frozen water pipe results in a lost run
that seldom can be made up. Plus he is a big morale boost
for me. Next fall he'll be in college. This will be a big change
for the Warren family. He has become a big asset to the
daily operations and taking care of Jennifer and Whitney.
He is so reliable and trustworthy, he seems years older than
18. His demeanor will serve him well as he steps away from
the 'nest'. I feel honored he is my son.

Well it is almost daylight and time to go out the door
once again for a 12-15 hour day and many miles. The forest
is completely different in winter. The snow is heavy on the
trees. The silence is everywhere. Often you run 50 miles
without seeing another human, sometimes without even
seeing a recent track by human, snowmobile or animal. But
the ravens are always out and talk to us often. I'd leave food
for them if I knew how.

Jim, January 10: The Tahquamenon Country Sled Dog Race is history. The nice thing is it runs literally though our back yard. Everyone but me ran dogs and had a great day. We viewed the race as a special training run and kept our competitive natures under control.

Chris ran the A team dogs, those that are destined for Iditarod, in the 60 mile 12 dog class. This was his first competition with 12 dogs and he focused on a technically clean run and pocketed his competitive nature. He finished 8th with both he and the dogs looking very professional.

Whitney ran in the 6 dog sportsman class. She had a good run but off the pace from her run of 2003 when she finished 4th, only 1 second behind Chris. She is still fuming a year later.

Jennifer ran a team of puppies in the 4 dog class and was pleased with her performance.

Today was a day to remember. It was a nice family outing in the snow with our dogs. There were a lot of smiling faces.

Jim, January 12: I came home with the family after the Tahquamenon race. It was so different sleeping in a bed I tossed and turned all night. But it was comforting to listen to Jennifer's breathing as she slept beside me. Chris and Whit were sleeping in the rooms down the hall. Home! What a luxury. I also heard the cars driving down the roadway. It is getting too crowded here for me.

Jim, January 19: The dogs are incredible! I returned this afternoon about 4 pm from back to back runs totaling about 120 miles. I left here with teams from Alcan Kennel (Al Hardman) driven by Jim Conner and Gregg Hickmann. We awoke about 5 am and after a hearty breakfast we went

into the 8 inches of new snow and 5 degrees to prepare
the teams for departure. Rod and Jason were running
snowmobiles towing a small groomer to break out the trail.
The lake effect snow was falling heavily with stiff northwest
winds. Those are the conditions that create whiteouts. The
last minute we modified our route plans to keep away from
the open plains area of Barfield Lakes where the trail could
be impossible to find in the blowing snow.

My dogs were really fired. I braked heavily for the first 15
miles to be sure they wouldn't overheat. They just wanted
to run fast and far. We went along the Lake Superior shore
where snowmobile traffic would have the trail somewhat
open. The wind off the lake was bad. The breakers were
8-12 feet and roaring into the heavy ice shelf protecting the
beach. I could only see a few yards out to sea. The white
tops of the breakers blended into the heavy snowfall. It was
hard to imagine this is the same lake where families walked
with children and dogs in the summer sunshine. Today the
ice pellets that formed from the spray off of the waves were
blasting us like a sandblaster. The dogs were picking their
way across 4 foot drifts, jumping off one side only to try to
claw their way up another. Fortunately the trail took a turn
back into the protection of the forest within a mile or so.
Better! The big lake is spooky, even in the daylight.

But the dogs were incredible. As the miles went by I
marveled at the muscular little bodies moving efficiently
in line. No wasted motion. Tails were not wagging but they
were having fun. Occasionally one would cock an ear back
at me. At times one would look back just to be sure I was
still their. Ruby reached over and gave Beta a kiss behind
the ear. He doesn't like that but she still teases him. Alto
barked once at Peg. Wonder what he said. She ignored him.

The miles go by quickly. We stop at two hour intervals for a quick dog snack. I allow 3 minutes.

At about 10 miles out of Al's cabin a few of the dogs seemed to notice and began picking up the pace. When we were about 5 miles out they started to really pick up the pace. I estimated we hade already gone 60 miles, 6 hours, and they knew we were getting close. On the last mile they were running hard. The narrow trail into Al's was little more than a 3 foot deep rut in the snow. The trees were moving past too fast for safety. It was time to drive the sled and hold on because they were in control. I hooked down outside the cabin and practiced my checkpoint routine. In 35 minutes I had the dogs bedded on straw, and fed. I spent a little more time to work on their feet to be sure all was OK. When I walked away they were resting and looking much like 'puddles of fur on straw'. The falling snow had already covered them. They will be ready to do it all over again in a few hours. I am still amazed at these tough little dogs. They are incredible creatures!

Jim, January 20: Temperature about 10F. I planned to work on the plumbing since I still had no water from the well or no drains. A shower is becoming a priority. So I crawled under the cabin and started drilling holes in plastic piping to finish a diagnosis. I cut out the blocked drain pipe and thawed it in hot water from melted snow, then reconnected it with duct tape. When testing I was pleasantly surprised to find the well had thawed too. Everything is working, yeaaaaaah! I showered! This is a good day.

I should have been cold laying under the cabin in the dirt working on piping at 10 degrees but I was sweating. Later, I discovered I had not turned on the power so I went out to the generator shed in my long underwear and boots.

I stopped in the driveway and said a few words to the dogs. Then I thought it doesn't seem so cold out here today. I checked the thermometer, it was still 10F. I guess I am getting conditioned too.

Jim, January 22: I am sitting by the fire here at SledDog Lodge waiting for Al Hardman and Gregg Hickmann who were to arrive by 4pm. It is 9pm now. They were running two 16 dog teams the 55 miles from Al's with a couple of people running snowmobiles to break out the trail. The wind and snow was brutal today. Wind chill is about minus 20 degrees now and is expected to drop another 20 tonight. The plan was for Al and Greg to get in here, rest the dogs a few hours then run a 40 mile loop back to here to rest again. Then we were going to run back to Al's. The objective was to introduce shortened rests to observe which dogs recover best. Those will be on the "A" team destined for Iditarod.

I am a little worried they hit white-outs in the Barfield Lakes area. It is a large plain with only sparse trees. I have been lost out there alone, at night, in the drifting snow. When you get off the trail the sled bogs down in the deep snow. It is almost impossible to keep going unless you find the trail. The trail markers are too far apart. I hope they are OK. At least there are 4 of them. I was alone.

They have been on the trail for almost 12 hours. It usually takes about 6. Something has happened. But this is the kind of weather you have to be able to handle to run distance sled dog races. I hear snowmobiles. Yea!

The Final Preparations

Chris, January 23: I just got here at SledDog Lodge after a long, icy drive from our house. I started around noon and arrived here at 10:30. Normally, the drive is just over 4 hours, not ten and a half. I finished my credit requirements at high school yesterday and walked out the door. I'm not going back. I have worked with the school for the past two years to graduate early. While I'm not technically graduated, I'm free. That's all that matters at the moment. The treacherous highway to the cabin was nerve wracking, but I'm done and now I can sleep well tonight. Tomorrow, a new chapter begins in my life. I look forward to it

Jim, January 24: Chris is here at SledDog Lodge. Things are looking up. We can work together to get the final 400 miles on the dogs. He is a good companion. I am a fortunate man to have a son like Chris.

We ran the full 16 dog team this morning on a 40 mile run north past Browns Lake and then South down Maple Block. It is a good and fun trail in beautiful pine and hardwood forests. The sky was blue with no wind and temps were about zero. A perfect day!

The dogs are incredibly strong. A hardened and conditioned 16 dog team has awesome, sometimes frightening power. I asked Chris to watch the team while I took the snowmobile and checked out a critical part of the trail ahead. I returned to find the team several hundred yards down the trail from where I left them. Chris explained the team pulled the tree over that I had hooked the snow hook around. He had a hard time getting them stopped. I offered to have him drive the team for awhile. He said, "Not these idiots!" So I took over the team and we prepared to leave. Things were about to become ugly.

I pulled the first snow hook and the team bolted ahead dragging the remaining snow hook through the snow at full speed. I was bending down searching for the second hook moving under the snow when it hooked firmly into a log buried under the snow. Instantly I found myself flying through the air and I landed under the back feet of the wheel dogs. In a panic fearing the sled and remaining snow hook lunging toward me I was grabbing for anything I could to be sure I was dragged too. I fear the sharp hook. It could kill you if it caught into you just right. But fortunately the snow hook was firmly hooked on the log. I remember as I sat up in the snow the 16 pairs of eyes looking at me with a look that said, "what in the world are you doing up here laying in the snow under the dogs?" A quick survey of our situation revealed a broken sled stanchion but still a serviceable sled.

As training runs go, this was a good run. The dogs were strong. And this is a good day. I am so happy Chris is here.

Jim, January 27: We are loading the dogs this morning and heading home to finalize the shipping of our drop bags. The Mad Cow scare has messed up the shipping of beef through Canada so we are shipping alternate route through Washington State and up the coast. But the shipping date suddenly tightened so we have to leave early.

Drop bag assembly is a large task with no forgiveness. What we load this weekend will be what we use for the entire two weeks on the trail. The success or failure of all this effort and money hangs on what we have in those bags. Fortunately the help of Al Hardman with information makes this much easier and less risky. I am thankful for his help.

I have an unusual situation. The emerging trend is to feed only kibble on the trail. Top Mushers Jeff King and Martin Buser both supported this during the Rookie meeting. This is contrary to conventional wisdom of feeding a variety of raw meat along with the kibble. So knowing there is risk we are departing from the traditional feeding of meat. I am a little nervous about maintaining hydration but will work on that during the final training runs in February. The advantage of feeding only kibble is that it simplifies many steps in the feeding process saving time. Time translates into distance and rest, both are good, real good.

Jim, February 3: 12:30 a.m. at SledDog Lodge. The drop bags were shipped two days ago. What a big job to get them together. Today started at 5:30 am at home doing income taxes. We got on the road at 3:30. When we drove through the town of Paradise, MI, we noted the snow piles were higher than most houses. We stopped at the gas station to get some coffee and found a rebuilt snowmobile engine for sale; in the grocery store! We got in the truck and headed towards the cabin in snow squalls of varying degree. We luckily were able to drive into the driveway and get all the way to the cabin. Taking the 25 dogs to the yard was tough in the 15 inches of new snow. It was a long drive in the snow but finally we are back at SledDog Lodge for the last 9 days of Iditarod training.

Tomorrow and the following 8 days will see focused training to ensure the mental conditioning of the dogs is adequate. We will run a series of 40 to 60 mile legs combining 2 to 3 legs to total maybe 150 miles.

I have the sense tonight that we are much closer to our objective. From this point forward, every breath, every step, everything will be focused on arriving in Nome with a healthy team and proud of the way we did it. I expect it will require our sweat, our heart and our soul. There will be risk, maybe a lot of risk. There will be obstacles, surprises, pain and disappointments. But we are well trained, committed, and able to meet the challenge.

I have assembled a detailed race plan that targets a 12-14 day elapsed time. Twelve days would be regarded as a 'best time' run. With the overriding objective to finish and learn, the plan includes giving the dogs longer rests as insurance. On a journey such as this there is almost certain to be surprises that will cost time. Managing these surprises is a big part of the learning. Finishing anywhere in the 12-14 day window will be considered success.

The team has several dogs that have been to Nome. This is a big advantage. The veterans hold back knowing that they'll need some reserve to go the distance. But, the youngsters just want to run and run. This mixture should make an interesting run. Hope I can keep them slow enough!

The driver is no stranger to the wilderness, or to endurance racing with its characteristic fatigue and emotional ups and downs. However, the dogs are better than the driver. I will count on them to pull us through when things get ugly. They will count on me to manage the runs and keep us on track. This is more of a team effort than most understand. The dogs have become much more than dogs to me. They are my friends, bound together by a common destiny. We speak in many ways but seldom with words.

Time to sleep, tomorrow will bring more challenges.

Jim, February 4: Dawn crept in finding me awake and worrying. The cost of this adventure has mounted and will consume the budget and then some. Just the materials for the shipping boxes for the drop bags cost over $600. All this is no surprise but still is weighing on me this morning. The help and encouragement of friends has been most appreciated.

It was nice to meet many friends at the Mackinaw Mush's dinner concert with Hobo Jim. It was a big lift for me. But I was reminded at how poor my hearing has become. I had to ask people to repeat often and then found myself reading their lips to ensure understanding. I have been a candidate for a hearing aid for quite a while but have resisted. I just don't want one more thing to have to fuss with. Could there be a vanity factor too? Yes. Regardless, I have to hear better so will have to get a hearing aid this summer.

I hear Chris talking in his sleep. Even the smell of coffee didn't wake him today. I'd better wake him. We have a ton of things to do other than running dogs. The dog houses are buried so deeply in the snow that some of the dogs can't get in the door and had to sleep in the snow. We have to dig and jerk the houses out of the snow. Even the snow in the dog circles is to the top of the 3 ½ foot posts.

Jim, February 6: Before dawn I found myself looking out the window at the 4 feet of snow on the ground with more snow hanging in the tall pines. It was a classic picture and could have been used for a Christmas card. We are near the end of our training time here. It has been an incredible amount of work, sweat, and aching joints. But, the time is right. I'm ready to move on to the trip to AK and then Iditarod.

Yesterday was eventful. When I took the 16 dog team

out of the yard Brutus didn't take the Gee to go down the driveway where Chris was waiting to escort us onto CR 500. Instead he dove into the heavy snow on the short trail leading to Swamp Lake Rd. The dogs were sinking out of sight in the deep snow. We made it to the road OK but Chris didn't show up behind us with the snowmobile. I began to worry. Things can and ALWAYS do happen when running dogs. In this remote and heavy snow country you have to be self sufficient. I turned north heading for the CR 414 crossing with no sign of Chris. The trail had about 15 inches of fresh snow. The team was running as strongly as when they started.

Finally I had radio contact with Chris. He was waiting at the CR414 crossing. The plan was to turn on CR414 and follow Chris to Tower Rd, an unplowed trail leading us to Whitefish Point. At the crossing, the noise of the snowmobile drowned out my commands to the leaders. The team dropped off the 4 foot bank onto CR414 and Brutus took a straight across course. He jumped carrying Pena with him and scrambled up the 5 foot bank on the opposite side. This was going to be a wild sled ride. The sled and I went airborne as we crested the bank. Wow! A trail hardened 16 dog team is awesome! Chris followed.

A short way down the trail Chris tried to pass us by following another snowmobile track a short distance off the main trail. Disaster! He got stuck. When the team saw him alongside of us they bolted off the trail in his direction. To help get us back on the trail he started running towards us in the deep snow and fell headlong. This startled the dogs; they stopped. Soon we were on our way. Chris was frantically trying to dig out the snowmobile. I had a wired dog team with no escort. It got worse.

I ran the team north down CR500 thinking there would

be more places to get them turned around; no small task with a team this large. Four miles later I found a place to hook down with the snow hook on a tree. I checked booties and stalled for time hoping to see Chris. I resolved to the fact he was probably stuck for the rest of the day. I was on my own.

When I pulled the knot on the snub rope it caught on a small branch making a big dilemma. I could break loose the knot but could never get back to the sled before the dogs bolted. Alone, I could little afford to have the team lost with hundreds of miles of trail for them to run. Finally I devised a scheme using the snow hook ropes tied to another tree. It took most of an hour but we finally were off.

I had a plan to circle around a 40 mile loop and run back by where the snowmobile was stuck. When we got on CR 412 the snow drifts were pretty deep. It got worse. Soon we were running through 10 foot drifts. Then downwind of a clear cut the drifts were higher than houses. We kept going, knowing that we were only a mile from a plowed road. Then, along a big clear cut area I looked ahead and saw a half mile of drifts higher than big houses. My heart sank.

Then the team got stuck and we weren't even in a big drift. I could see a lot of noses and tails sticking out of the deep snow. They were all looking at me. I found a tree to hook to and began tromping the snow down along side of the team preparing for a turn-around. I grabbed the leaders and began running back alongside of the team. I got about 20 feet when I couldn't pull them anymore. When I looked back both Pepsi and Dell had decided they wanted to keep going ahead and were pulling ahead as hard as they could. Those are the most stupid dogs I have ever seen. You can count on them doing something incredibly stupid at the worst time.

We got turned around but Pepsi and Dell created enough confusion that a major dog tangle occurred. After an hour, a lot of sweat, and a dog bite on my hand we were ready to go again. We backtracked heading for the cabin.

Chris had walked the 2 ½ miles back to the cabin to get shovels and a winch. He had gotten out of the first problem only to get stuck farther away from the trail. We worked until after dark to free the snowmobile.

So, it all ended well. There were no major injuries. My hand is sore from the dog bite. Chris is complaining of very sore muscles.

That is the way it is at training camp. If you are still alive, and are healthy enough to head out again the next day, it was a good day.

Jim, February 7: Chris and I are back at SledDog Lodge after a 110 mile trip that took us to Grand Marais, then to the cabin of Al Hardman north of McMillan. We left at 4pm yesterday and were making good time when the dogs started to act up. I changed dog positions, switched out leaders, and was becoming frustrated when we finally noticed their protective booties were allowing snow to accumulate inside causing them pain. Soon we started checking and changing booties about every 5 miles. They picked up the pace and ran hard for the last 10 miles into Al's. As the race gets closer I am getting worried about these dogs being to fast too be safe.

Later, upon pulling the snow hook leaving Al's, the dogs rocketed down his driveway and with no warning took a 90 degree turn left into his dog yard causing me to barrel-roll the sled. With me dragging behind the sled, they ran at full speed through one side of the dog yard, then turned and ran back through the other side of the dog-yard. With all of Al's dogs in an uproar, they finally departed on a completely different trail than I'd intended. What in the world had gotten into them? I could have been mad at them or at the least embarrassed but thought better of it.

On the leg back we met 8-10 snowmobiles traveling much too fast. The first passed us head-on like a bullet making a big cloud of snow. Out of the cloud came another, and another. They began braking and swerving dangerously close to us. Chris was running escort ahead of the dog team with the snowmobile. One of the swerving snowmobiles clipped his cargo sled and broke the hitch. One more came out of the snow cloud at 50 plus MPH. He got sideways as he passed Chris and then came straight at me and the sled. For a moment it looked like he would slice my sled in two lengthwise. I jumped to the right runner. He missed! Just after he rocketed past me there as a loud crash. I presumed he hit one of the snowmobiles that had slowed.

I didn't dare look back. We were still running in the snow cloud and I could hear more coming. When I finally looked back I saw what looked like pieces of snowmobile scattered in the trail and bodies on the snow. With still more snowmobiles coming at us I didn't dare try to stop to give aid. It was the lesser risk to keep the dogs moving and on the far right side of the trail.

It was a sobering experience. Fortunately we were unscathed. There is more risk to this activity than meets the eye. My prayers and thoughts are with those who were not as fortunate.

Chris, February 7: We just got back from a 100 mile loop over to Al Hardman's cabin. The trip was pretty much uneventful until we started to come home. First the dogs took a scenic tour of Al's Dog yard. They went out of it one way, turned around, went through it again in the other direction, and then took off in a direction that was the complete opposite of our intended direction. We were able to handle the course shift okay, and then things got worse. As we were traveling down a county road, marked as snowmobile trail, a group of 8 to12 snowmobiles came blasting around a corner. Those guys had to be traveling near 60 mph when I met the first one. They tried to slow down for the dogs but it was too little, too late. The first guys were able to slow down and actually almost stop. The only problem was that the ones behind them couldn't see, on account of the snow clouds in front of them. One came within inches of my dad's sled. Immediately after he went by, my dad heard a loud crash. He couldn't look back because he still had to deal with the snowmobiles ahead of him. He couldn't stop because the dogs were still too fresh. When he finally could look back, he saw pieces of snowmobile everywhere and bodies on the ground. I sincerely hope no one was killed or seriously injured.

After that, the rest of the trip was relatively uneventful. We got home safe and sound. Fortunately, we still had enough daylight to feed dogs and clip toenails.

Today is the first day I that have had a chance to use the computer before I am too tired to think. I have been finished with high school for almost three weeks now and I have spent every minute of it, except the first day of celebration, working with the dogs. As tired as I am at the end of the day here, I am nowhere near the level of fatigue that I was during school. Eight hour days at school, and then another four or five hours of homework is a lot of work. It was especially demanding when I had to manage our Christmas Tree Farm while my dad was at the Iditarod Rookies Meeting, and was captain for my school's varsity basketball team. There were a lot of 20-hour days in December.

These past few weeks however have been nothing but pleasure for me. Sure, handling dogs can be one of the hardest things to do physically, but where else can you find that many unconditional friends to work with. The dogs are their own reward for me. Their wagging tails and smiling faces can make even the worst runs seem trivial in nature.

I'm glad that I can be up here with my dad. In the few short weeks I have been here, his energy level and overall morale have improved significantly. He smiles more, talks to the dogs more, and gets a lot more done. I feel privileged to share in his dream of running the Iditarod, and right now I am just trying to keep all the pieces moving in the same direction (he is sometimes a little forgetful of small details, like musher food). On an unrelated note where else, other than Michigan's Upper Peninsula, can you walk into the gas station/ pizza place/ mini hardware store and find a rebuilt snowmobile engine for sale. It struck me that this is a totally different world from the rest of the state. While I was drinking my coffee later that evening I wondered, where else will my life lead me in the next year?

Chris, February 9: Today was a good day. We ran 50 miles in a loop that takes us to the northeast and the sun was shining all day. Two months ago, I would have said 50 miles was a long way on a dog sled. Today, it still is a long way, but it is far more manageable than I would have guessed. The dogs were phenomenal today. Swen, an all star two year old shined. He has been sidelined for almost a month and a half with a muscle tear in his left leg, and today he ran 50 miles and scarcely missed a beat. He worked his heart out and was still standing in harness and wanting to play with me as I tried to put a salve on his sore leg. What a dog! He is definitely my favorite, no questions asked. If he turns out not to be a sled dog due to injury then I will definitely keep him as a pet.

I am really enjoying my time spent up here because the concept of time doesn't really exist. It seems strange, but life is really pleasurable when you can live life according to the natural rhythms of day and night. The bells that drive high school students don't exist in any form. It is so relaxing to live at your own pace, rather than the clock that drives students and the rest of the civilized world.

Jim and 16 Dog Team Training

Jim, February 10: 6 am: Sitting in front of the wood

burner drinking my coffee this morning my head is swirling with last minute things that must be done before we depart for Alaska next week. What dogs to take; do I have enough dog food for the left behind dogs; how do I get it all home in one trip; getting behind on emails and phone messages; and on and on. I guess it comes with the territory.

Yesterday's 51-mile run to Whitefish Point was superb. The 16 dogs took me out of the yard like a rocket, off the 4 foot drop into the plowed driveway, and out to CR 500 where Chris was waiting to ensure a safe entrance onto the roadway. As the team dashed the two miles to Tower, an unplowed road, I marveled at the muscular bodies, now in full winter coat, moving rhythmically. The team looked well matched, strong, and ready. The power of a trail hardened team is awesome. I was standing on full brake and could only slow to maybe 15 mph. There was no doubt in my mind that if I was going with them then I'd better hold on tight.

Weather was warm and sunny, 25 degrees. Normally this would be good news but for sled dogs this was weather to endure; too hot. I nearly shortened the planned run but after a couple of 5 minute stops to cool they seemed to find a speed that would accommodate the conditions. This is good. They need to learn how to deal with the heat. We ran the entire 51 miles in 6 hour flat with numerous bootie stops, a very good run in hot conditions.

Chris has learned what dog handling/training is like. You get up and do chores to get ready for the run. You run the team, now taking from 6 to 20 hours. Back in the dog yard the first thing you do is feed, check all dog feet and medicate the sore ones, massage and check all dogs for soreness, bring one or two inside for the night if severe muscle strain. Then you have time for yourself to eat, maybe shower, and if you can hold off the fatigue you can take care of correspondence. The first priority is the family. A call home is a welcomed time but the warmth of the wood heater makes it impossible to stay awake. You ignore the muscle and joint soreness that is inevitable when dealing with deep snow. You have taken better care of the dogs than you have of yourself. You get up early the next day and do it all again, and again.

This morning I am surprised to find my hands swollen and stiff; barely able to handle the keyboard. I had run the dogs yesterday without gloves. Maybe that is more exposure than one thinks. I'll try to wear gloves and cool my body other ways.

This may be the last regular entry to the web journal since we will be leaving SledDog Lodge by Friday. We will then depart for AK on Tues or Weds of next week. We will travel with the computer so will still make entries but they may not get posted regularly. Chris hopes to carry the computer with him on the trail to make progress reports where ever he is. It should be an adventure!

Jim, February 11: Sitting by the toasty wood heater this evening I am satisfied. We are finished with dog training. I've put my sweat, my heart and my soul in the preparation of these dogs. The dogs have 1400-1700 training miles. Our recent series of runs totaling about 300 miles demonstrate a solid team, well condition, well trained, and ready for Iditarod. Even better, many of them have valuable experience having run Iditarod in the kennels of Jeff King and Linwood Fiedler.

So, at this point the dogs are probably better than the musher. That was the plan. I wanted and sought out the best dogs I could buy. I think it was worth it. So tonight I am satisfied and very tired!

Jim, February 12: 6 am: We are leaving SledDog Lodge today and have an early start. The dog yard, that had been so full of action and noise, will again fall silent and become blanketed by the unending snow and cold. The local coyotes will come in and eat any food they can find. They are so hungry they even clean up any dog poop we missed. They must be hungry!

Back at home Chris and I will have to become re-accustomed to little things taken for granted such as the thermostat controlling indoor temperature and bed sheets instead of sleeping bags. Although SledDog Lodge has a thermostat we used the wood heater allowing temps to get down low during the night. Early morning ritual was to light the gas lamps, fire up the wood heater, pull on my fleece garments and foam boot liners, then fire up the computer. After spending most of the time outdoors the cool indoors was preferred. But I did sit by the wood heater after showering. Nice.

Then we will be on the road with the dogs heading for Alaska, a long trip, very long.

Chris, February 15: This last weekend was one to remember. For their wedding anniversary, my dad put my mom on the back of a sled behind six Iditarod dogs and sent her off into the sunset. No, really, he actually did that. This is the last weekend before we leave for Alaska, so we went to the Pellston Icebox Sleddog race. My mom entered herself in the six dog class and my sister in the eight dog class during Christmas break and was bound and determined to go. My dad and I did our best to make it so that the ladies only had to show up, get on the sled, and ride away. We did all the chores, Mom and Whitney had all the fun.

It was worth it though. My mom has been training and

exercising for more than a year to be able to run dogs. This was the first time since she had her hamstring torn in two by an accident that she was able to ride a dogsled for 25 miles. The fact that she had a clean, smooth run is nothing short of remarkable. She didn't do well in the standings, but her joy at finishing definitely outweighed her disappointment.

Whitney had a phenomenal run. She stepped on the sled at the start line and her first word, after looking at her barking and lunging team was "Whoa!" I have been on quite a few fast rides and I knew, as I watched her team accelerate into the distance, that she was either going to spend a lot of time dragging behind the sled, or she would have a ride to remember. When we saw her team an hour later, they were still running as hard as when they left the start chute. When Whitney finished the race, she started talking excitedly about her run. "They were running like they stole something!" she said, "They never even slowed down!" This is all the more impressive if you know that the race was 40 miles long. When all was said and done, Whitney won fifth place, and $75, amongst some of the best teams in the Midwest. It's the first time she won money and she will be almost intolerable for a few days. Good for her.

I give my dad a lot of credit. He gave the two most important women in his life wonderful gifts. Both Mom and Whitney had a fun, relaxing weekend. Whitney felt the thrill of a rocket-fast team and the pride of having done well; Mom had the satisfaction that comes with achieving long term personal goals and gained a new confidence in her abilities. I'm just glad I could help.

Whitney: Finish at Pellston Icebox Race

We leave for Alaska in a few days. Unlike the last month of training however, there are no do-overs. My last year-and-a-half of school was focused on getting to this point, and now that I am here, my perspective is frightening. When I first decided to go through with this adventure it was a long way away and I could only see how great it is, like a mountain at a distance. Now that I am standing at the base, ready to climb up, I can see the hard jagged lines of the mountain before me. Don't get me wrong, I am ready to go. I am confident in my ability to do what I need to do. The anxiety that I am feeling is natural whenever you step outside of your comfort zone. However, these last few days have illuminated me as to why people say "Wow, that's so cool, I wish I could go." This is a real adventure. I feel really fortunate to go and I only hope that things go well.

Heading North

Chris, February 18: After a late start we finally got going. We packed our bags and got ready for today, and yet, we still didn't leave until 2:00 in the afternoon. Spending half a day fixing my dad's sled didn't help. I am not looking forward to the trip to Alaska. I have been with my father before on road trips before races and he is just way too serious a lot of the time

Note: This is the second entry for today. I think I will attend Purdue University. Not because of its superior academics, but because of its proximity to my grandparents' house. We got here at 10:30 tonight and what do you know, Grandma threw in some roast beef, potatoes, and carrots in the microwave. I have never had better roast beef in my life. Sorry Mom! Then Grandma walked out with a pumpkin pie and chocolate chip cookies with walnuts! My favorites! That pie was the best pumpkin pie I think I have ever had, sorry again Mom. Things are looking up for the rest of the trip so I am going to bed and I will finally post this in the morning.

Chris, February 21: After 4 hard days of driving we made it across the Canadian border this evening. After we had left Grandma's house we headed west, through Iowa, South Dakota, Wyoming and Montana. I have never seen so much pretty country! From the hills in the Badlands to the northernmost areas of Montana, the trip was beautiful. The huge expanses of open prairie, miles upon miles of mountains, and expansive valley's are good for me. There is something about the wide open spaces and big sky that lets me feel peace of mind and speaks to my soul. I didn't even mind when I wound up driving for 6 hours straight today. I remember now why I was so excited about the possibility of going to Montana Tech. This land calls to me. I will live here someday.

Jim, February 25: 5 am; Haines Junction, Yukon Territory: This is the 8th day on the road. We have been traveling 11-12 hours a day. Yesterday we traveled 16 hours with the last 8 hours on slippery mountain roads. The truck is marvelous and handles well. The 22 foot trailer, that contains our dogs and supplies, IS NOT the best rig to be traveling with on winter roadways in the mountains. Some of the down hill sections have been white knuckle rides, especially in the dark during a storm.

We have been getting up at 5:30 each day. After a quick shower we take care of the dogs. We perform what we call a dog drop. Each of the 24 dogs is taken out of its comfortable warm box and is connected by a short drop chain to the outside of the trailer. They are excited and happy to be out and stretch and wiggle a lot. We feed them and give each a little attention before putting them back in their box. After a quick continental breakfast at the motel we are on the road. By 9am we have to stop and drop the dogs again. For lunch we make a sandwich for ourselves from our cooler but never stop driving. At 1 or 2 pm we drop dogs again plus do our afternoon watering. Two hours later we stop and drop again. Four hours after that we drop dogs for the last time that day. They are ready to overnight in their boxes. A good dog drop takes about 20 minutes, although our record for 24 dogs is 13 minutes.

We are taking care to get at least one good meal per day

for ourselves but have been so tired at the end of the days travel we sometimes have skipped eating. Some days our cooler with its supply of food has been like our best friend. The dogs are getting tired of traveling and so are we. We should be in Anchorage tomorrow.

The scenery is spectacular. The trouble is there is so much of it. We've seen along the roadway buffalo, moose, caribou, wolves, coyotes, elk, and had a very rare sighting of a wolverine.

The alarm clock has been going off for about 5 minutes and Chris is still sleeping. I think he needs a day off but we have over 700 miles of mountain roads ahead to get to Anchorage. Then we'll rest!

The day of travel started well before dawn. The sound of the Chevy diesel working against the mountain roadway in the unending cold has become almost musical. The icy roadway shows in our headlights but little else is visible. It seems we are the only inhabitants in the entire Yukon Territory. Breakfast today is a very large chocolate chip cookie frozen solid from the cold in the truck overnight. The temperature outside is minus 10. I am not amused to find my water bottle solidly frozen and no way to wash down the last of the cookie. I wonder how the early people who lived here found water to drink during winter.

Even before first light the snow covered mountain to our left starts to glow with the soft light of the dawn. It is gigantic. Soon the entire range is glowing like an expensive jewel. Then the sparse tundra forest of the high plateau slowly becomes visible. Chris is beside himself watching the dawn arrive in the most stunning landscape in the world. He complains the camera could never capture the view. He finally says, "I'll just record this with my memory." "I wish Mom and Whit could see this!" We continued in silence except for the sound of the Chevy diesel. Dawn was a very special treat for us and a kind of payment for our days of hard travel.

Somewhere on the ALCAN Hwy

Chris, February 25: I saw a sunrise today. A simple event to be sure, but we have been headed northwest for so long the only thing I have seen is broad daylight, sunsets, and one snowstorm in the middle of the night. Sunrise this morning was special. In addition to the sun coming over the mountains in the east, I got to see alpenglow for the first time in my life. The alpenglow is a really spectacular effect. During the early morning or late evening, when the sunlight causes the world to soften, the first, or last, bit of direct sunlight hits a mountain peak covered in snow. Rather than being a bright white, or yellow, the mountain casts an orange glow that looks like firelight. I managed to get a picture, but I need to use some editing software to make it look the way it did this morning.

The mountains on the northern edge of Canada are

really beautiful. It has been so cold here for so long that the occasional power line is covered in an inch of ice. The trees are covered in snow and frost that has been there for who knows how long. The valleys in these mountains are cold enough that the air moisture condenses and forms a dense fog. The snow is made all the more beautiful by the sunshine (except where it's foggy). Come to think of it, we have had sunny skies every day on our way up here. The one snowstorm we did have happened at night and it screwed up the roads for two days.

The days that we have spent on the road have made us hardened travelers. We woke up at 6:00 this morning, fed dogs, checked out of the hotel, and were on the road eating cinnamon rolls by 6:45. We have averaged 12 hours a day driving up here and it doesn't even bother me anymore. Interestingly enough I had almost constant cell phone coverage until Edmonton. After that though, I haven't had any, except for about 30 seconds when a lost radio wave hit my antenna.

We are approaching the US Customs into Alaska so I better put this away. I hope to update again soon, bye.

In the Yukon Territory

Chris, February 26: We have to be just a little crazy. The past two days we have been remarking how warm it is outside when we are dropping dogs. Then we get inside the truck and look at the thermometer, it is 10 degrees. This morning we thought of as "a little cool" while we were working; the thermometer read 10 below zero. Remarkable as that is, there are other strange things that happen when your body adjusts to the cold. I don't notice it except for little things, like working without gloves at 20 degrees, or being too warm in a room that is 65.

We will arrive at our destination today after eight and a half days of driving. It's about time. I don't mind driving in the truck, the seats are really comfortable, but I'm just sick and tired of staring at the scenery and not having much better to do, I need to do something different. The routine of travel is almost as bad as living according to bells during school. I am looking forward to having a chance to do laundry and prepare for the race. Fortunately, my grandma gave me money for lodging during our travels. I really have appreciated the hot shower and daily good meal. Tomorrow begins a new chapter in this journey.

Jim, February 26: We arrived in Wasilla, AK, today after 95 hours of driving. The last 1200 miles of ice covered mountain roadway has taken a toll on us. We are tired. My teeth hurt from clenching them for hours on end on the slippery mountain highway. But we arrived safely. The dogs are bedded in the Kwik Kard storage area and are very happy to be out of their boxes. I am very tired and need a couple of days to regain my sense of humor. Enough said.

We are fortunate to be staying in the home of Mark Conrad, his wife Nina and daughter Amanda. Mark grew up nearby my hometown in Midland, MI, and is now pastor of a Methodist church in Wasilla. Mark is a musher and lives almost on the Iditarod dog trail running out of Wasilla going to Knik. They are a great people and it is a special treat to stay with them.

Pre-Race Jitters

Jim, February 27: Today begins the hectic time of pre-race activities. We will pamper the dogs with special food and lots of attention. They need to have a special wormer furnished by Iditarod folks. Monday they will all have blood drawn and an EKG as part of a complete physical. Wednesday they will be checked by the Iditarod vet teams.

As for us, today we meet with Mary Pemberton of AP out of Anchorage and a photographer. She is doing a story on an Iditarod musher. Then we have dozens of items to attend to including packing my sled in detail including the pockets of my trail clothing. Nothing will be overlooked because when we leave here in a few days I want no careless omission to be an obstacle to the success of these dogs.

There are rumors that the second start will be out of Willow instead of the customary Wasilla because of the lack of snow. When I was here at the rookie meeting in December there was a lot of snow. Today, it looks like there has been a spring thaw. Other than in the woods there is no snow. If we start out of Willow it means I will have to deal with a hot 16 dog team alone with no second sled. That is a little unnerving considering the passing that may be involved with nearly a hundred teams starting on two minute intervals.

I am getting anxious to start. I want to see this spectacular country up close. My nagging fear is that the dogs may catch a virus and cause us to loose a lot of time. Also I think we have 3, perhaps 4, females coming into heat which may be handful of problems. During training we train them normally when in heat as part of the training to learn to deal with it just like any other trail condition. I guess we will have to take what comes. We will focus every breath and step on getting to Nome.

Chris just came out of the shower and asked, "What are we doing for breakfast?" While looking out of Conrad's window facing the woods and dog yard he exclaimed, "There is a Moose, two of them! This is Alaska!"

Jim, February 28: I am having trouble getting to sleep tonight so thought I would write a little. A traffic incident just South of the Iditarod Headquarters has been triggering memories of a much worse incident I encountered a couple of months back.

Tonight driving back about a mile past Iditarod Headquarters on Goose Bay Road, we came upon a serious road crash. I saw the T-bone crash; the cars sliding then come to rest. Ahead on the debris strewn roadway was a small pickup with the right side heavily damaged with the occupant partially out of the broken window. I pulled up with my truck blocking traffic to provide some protection for Chris and me. I grabbed my Fire Department medical bag and we went to assess the situation. I quickly did an IPS (Initial Patient Survey) on the most seriously injured. He was lucid but had sustained a heavy blow in the Rt. side. Major bones and limbs were angulated properly and operable but pulse and visuals indicated shock. I monitored him for a few seconds but could not assess stability. He was in trouble, serious trouble.

A cell phone was thrust in my face by someone who said the 911 Dispatcher wants to talk to a medic. The dispatcher wanted to know the number and severity of injuries.

Before I responded I went quickly to the other vehicle and observed the driver standing outside the vehicle on the passenger side. The lady inside looked to be pregnant. I asked, "Are you alright Ma'am; are you pregnant?" She was pregnant and immediately became the priority of a triage situation.

As soon as local medical and fire personnel arrived I turned over the work to them and went back to my truck. The Incident Commander thanked me for my help. I briefly looked around the accident scene and thought of the hundreds of times this is repeated. Now that I am not able to sleep I think more of what I have seen and have experienced as a Firefighter. The Medical First responders, Firefighters, and Police, many of them volunteers, come away from their comfortable warm homes to give aid to people whom they never new. They look so professional and knowledgeable. The truth is many are working out of their comfort zone. A big reason for this is emergency work in the field is always chaos and seldom the way it is portrayed in training. People are hurt and dying. You see the worst and best coming out in them. But the volunteers understand and are there giving the best aid they can; giving of themselves, sometimes more than they anticipated.

I think of the unusual bond there is between firefighters. They come from all walks of life, income levels and backgrounds. I've found them to be not uniformly moral, honest or upright people. They span the spectrum. But they come together when the alarm sounds and they work, sometimes at great personal risk, at times in very ugly conditions, to help someone who they never knew and will probably never see again. There is always an emotional toll.

The next day, the local newspaper reported the death of the person in the truck and the birth of a baby.

Jim, March 3: The pre-race activities are wearing us down. I think both Chris and I are doing our best to get through it. The Iditarod folks are extremely efficient and pleasant to work with. They are a class-act of major proportion. They make it tolerable.

The dogs are feeling pretty poorly. Some are not eating with what looks to be some kind of intestinal bug. Maybe it is just the travel combined with the warm slushy weather. We need to get on the trail to work out these things. Both the dogs and driver need a lot more space and fresh air than we've been getting lately.

Chris, March 3: The past 6 days have been tedious. A minor virus appears to be going through the team. It isn't serious, but the dogs stopped eating for a couple days. Unfortunately, this came just after we gave the dogs the Iditarod-mandated worm medicine. The medicine was pretty rough on the dogs. Even Peg, who will eat just about anything you put in front of her, just kind of looked at the food and turned around. So after 3 or 4 days of not eating and feeling ill, they were really happy to get extra portions, and extra hugs, today.

The chores are just about done. All that remains of the prep-work is packing the sled, which my dad has to do; otherwise he won't know where things are. Thus, the only things that remain are scooping dog poop, feeding dogs, and killing time. I am getting really good at that last one. The tedium is manageable, but dealing with my dad is starting to get difficult. He is starting to become nervous about the race and he is running out of things to do. This is nothing new, but the amount of nervous energy is almost overwhelming.

While my dad is on the race trail, I will be hopping between a few checkpoints to get a look at what really happens at the checkpoints. I need to get in contact with a few people and get a hold of names and numbers for transport. Hopefully they can give me an idea as to where the towns with internet hookups are. That way I can contact people in the outside world. It would be a shame to wind up stuck in one checkpoint for a whole week with nothing to do but take pictures and read a book.

While I was still in school I helped direct several plays for the 5th and 6th grades. It was arguably the most hectic, least enjoyable part of my day. While I was doing it, I knew I would be glad to be gone. While I am glad that I don't have to deal with 40 kids on sugar highs after lunch, at least it was never boring. I am almost to the point of missing drama class, perhaps better called "Chaos Management", with the amount of dead time that I have to fill.

On a side note, the family I am staying with is wonderful. Mark Conrad, the father, is a Methodist minister who happens to run dogs. He and his family are preparing for a move to Arizona and as a result he is being forced to liquidate his kennel. He has several of Martin Buser's dogs, and due to the limited time he has, is trying to move them quickly. While I don't see our kennel purchasing dogs soon, I wish him luck with getting all of his business sorted out. Mrs. Conrad and Amanda are wonderful people. They are both great to talk to and they both have a great sense of humor.

Last night Mrs. Conrad invited me to come watch Amanda play in the Matanuska-Susitna Valley Honors Band. It was amazing! So amazing, in fact, I had goose bumps and shivers occasionally during the performance. After the show, we went to McDonalds for fries and then we went back to the house. After we got inside, Amanda promptly kicked my butt in a game of foosball. I don't remember what the score was, but I did quit before she reached 100 points (no that's not a typo).

We have to be leaving here at 6:45 tomorrow for a breakfast in Anchorage so I have to go.

Heading to NOME!!

Note from Jennifer: Chris kept up the journal on the website while the race was on. Jim's notes from the trail were added after he got into Nome. Chris and I received many e-mails during the race and some of them are included here

e-Mail: Mr. Warren, I am in Yokohoma, Japan. I was born in Flint Michigan and am over here for three years as a teacher's aide. Mrs. Ferry (a teacher from the 4th grade) has gotten her class involved in picking a musher and a rookie for the Iditarod 2004. I have chosen you as my rookie so "my money is on you." GO MICHIGAN! I was wondering if you have any pictures of the dogs, you and the team, etc. that you could e-mail me. Also the names of your dogs (please identify the lead dog's name). I realize that the 6th of March is soon at hand and you may not get this e-mail in time. We will be watching the race as close as we can. Best of luck, Patrick

e-Mail: Jennifer, My name is Cathy. I was a volunteer dog handler for Jim at the ceremonial start in Anchorage. I was holding onto the second dog on the right side in his line up. After emailing Chris, I found out the dogs name is Alto. He was a very excited dog! Here are a few pictures my mom took at the start in Anchorage. Please let me know how Jim and Alto are doing. Happy Trails, Cathy Christensen

Jim, Jennifer, Cathy at Anchorage Start

Whitney and Chris Having a Great Day

Chris, March 6: Wow, the past two days have been exciting. Yesterday was the ceremonial start in Anchorage. My dad drew number 73 out of 87 so we had to wait a long time, but it was definitely worth the extra hour or so. There were thousands of people walking around 4th Avenue, where the race starts. We finally harnessed and hooked up the dogs around 11:30 after waiting for 5 hours.

Our dogs were so strong that they required 14 people to hold them, and even with the braking power of two sleds it was a struggle! For safety, the Race Officials require that two drivers leave with the team at the Anchorage start. The added control of the team is necessary because of the large number of spectators and there is an Iditarider riding in the main sled. My dad graciously let Whitney and me ride the sled and the tag sled up to the start line.

As the announcer counted the seconds down from 10, my dad turned around, looked back at me on the tag sled, and flashed the biggest smile of his life. As we rocketed out of the start chute I couldn't help myself; I started laughing out of sheer elation. The sun was out, the dogs were strong, and the air was clean. The ten mile long ceremonial start was lined by thousands of people, all cheering and waving and smiling. The last two years of long nights, hard work, and frustration were worth it. There is something magical about riding a sled behind an Iditarod team on your way out of Anchorage. That feeling alone was worth even the 4000 mile road trip.

Anchorage Start

e-Mail: Jennifer, I have e-mailed Mr. Warren just before the race. I just wanted you to know that I am keeping him in my prayers and my favorite to win. I've read stories about him online (as Chris puts it, "He's tougher than even he thinks.") I am a Teacher's Aide in Japan for the next three years and the reason I've become so interested in the Iditarod is that Mrs. Ferry, (our 4th grade teacher) has gotten her students involved by picking a musher and rookie. She asked me to do the same. Being born in Michigan, I chose Mr. Warren as my Rookie. The more I read about him, the more he becomes a legend-in-his-own-time, in my eyes. May God guide him through the snow.

God speed to him, Patrick Councilor (Japan)
PS: I will keep up-to-date on Chris's Journal for news on the Iditarod. Do you know of a site that might give the latest updates on the race? Thank you

Chris, March 8: Whew, it's all over. My dad left the restart in Willow looking so relieved that he might fall asleep on the sled runners. Now that the dog work is over, for a few weeks anyway, I can focus on my own stuff. I leave for the Iditarod checkpoint town of McGrath tomorrow at 8:00 am. I'm looking forward to being on the trail. My dad, at the Skwentna checkpoint, left a message on my phone last night. He had to run the dogs almost 70 miles before they would settle down enough to rest. I am really happy for him. He seemed so excited over the phone.

The fatigue and stress of the last month have finally caught up with me. I am beginning to relax, which is a good thing. Mom misplaced the camera. Fortunately, I do have a backup. I will send pictures as soon as possible.

Christopher: "It Doesn't Get Any Better"

e-Mail: Jennifer, He's headed to Nome!

It is great to hear Jim is off and "running." Mike and I were watching the Outdoor Cable Channel and saw Jim being interviewed. His mom had a nice article written by Associated Press as well. We are all cheering him on. I'm glad you and Whitney were able to be there for the starts. What a thrill! Stay calm at home. Jim will be smart as he travels the trail.

Have a great day. I'll check your website for progress updates. Lynne e-Mail: Hello! I live just down Carter Road a short way from your home and have cut Christmas trees from your farm for years. I was thrilled to see that you have entered into such a wonderful adventure and am living my dream vicariously through you and your family. We have friends in Wasilla and have toured the beautiful state (briefly) twice, and in that time have come to love the idea of Alaska in all its splendor and majestic nobility. It is truly a humbling place. Somewhat like this race itself. After talking to mushers, it is truly in their blood and I can only hope to experience that kind of passion in my lifetime.

I just wish to pass on a bit of luck and good wishes to you and your family, and thank you for sharing your adventure with those of us who will never have the chance to experience something like this for ourselves. I look forward to hearing updates and about your story from the website and news media. All the Best! Thank You, Erin

Jim, Skwentna: After the official restart in Willow, the first section of the trail was smooth and fast. The dogs seemed to look for another then another team to pass. I was braking heavily but couldn't slow them enough. I had never seen them so wired. I was worried they would burn them selves out.

Heads, Tails Down and Running Hard

Brutus was living the dream of every sled dog; he was leading a world class team on the starting leg of the Iditarod. He was making the very best of the situation. When he spied a team ahead he would pull hard and steady to close the gap, even though I was braking hard trying to keep them slow to ensure no overheating. When close enough to think about passing he'd hit his harness with full power, tail and head down, looking much like a ball of fur. The team behind him responded to the call and added extra power. They took me through several fast passes and just kept on running. Brutus was at the top of his game and he knew it.

Brutus Closing on Team Ahead

Into Yentna, the first checkpoint, about 30 miles from the start, I thought I'd see if they would rest. Silly me! I stopped the team just short of the officials to let a team ahead clear. The leaders decided they wanted to take a 90 degree turn right, swinging the whole team and upending a lady standing alongside of the trail with her arms full of bags. Then to my complete embarrassment they decided they'd made a mistake and swung back, clothes-lining the lady again only this time from behind with no warning. She tumbled completely over in the snow and came up swearing. She instantly clamped her hands over her mouth and said no more.

In the parking area of the checkpoint I had to ask a person to stand on both of my snow hooks just to hold the dogs while I worked with the vets to check the team. The dogs were not going to wait, they wanted to run with or without me! I decided I'd better leave with them and run up the river to Skwentna the next checkpoint. To my total dismay on leaving they over-ran the 3 helpers who had to drop the lines and scramble out of the way. They proceeded to run over about a dozen marker stakes and tear out about 200 feet of marker ribbon denoting the resting area. With marker stakes and lots of plastic ribbon hanging all over the dogs we rocketed out of the checkpoint. I didn't look back; too embarrassed.

Into Skwentna, 75 miles from the start, the dogs were ready for a 6 hour rest and so was I.

e-Mail: Jennifer, Please thank Jim and Chris for their journal entries posted at the Warren Homestead Tree Farm web site. It is fun to learn the 'behind the scenes' stories of who, what, when and where about the Iditarod participants. At this point in the race Jim is at Skwenta.

Best wishes! E. Bieck

Jim and Full Team of 16 Dogs Near Skwentna

Jim, Finger Lakes: The dogs took me out of Skwentna checkpoint several hours before dawn. The trail was hard and fast, the air was clean, the stars were spectacular and all was as it should be. This was an enjoyable run. As dawn broke I could see the mountains of Alaska Range looming ahead with more mountains behind. This is spectacular country. It just doesn't get any better. We rested during the heat of the day in the checkpoint of Finger Lakes. The sun was almost too warm to sleep comfortably on the sled.

Jim, Rainy Pass: "All hell broke loose!" Out of Finger Lake we entered the first steep chute about a half mile downhill within 4 foot walls of snow. After careening down the hill it leveled for a moment and I notice a dog was missing, but before I could hook down we began another steep descent. Finally I hooked down and looked back up the trail for the dog. No dog! Then to my horror I noticed a tug line running backward under the sled. I jumped off and started digging under the front of the sled and found Peg motionless. I pulled her out but she was not breathing. I gave her two breaths (CPR) and started chest compressions. Suddenly she took a big gulp of air and began breathing. Whew! In a few minutes she was on her feet and back on the gangline, but I was worried. Soon it was evident she was unable to continue. I put her in one of our special dog bags so she could be secured comfortably on top of the sled. Unknown to me at the time, this was probably the worst place in the world to carry a 50 pound dog on top of the sled.

A short time later I noticed the Iditarod Trail Marker had a special warning in capital letters, "WATCH YOUR ASS!" I smiled at the irreverent humor. I had grown to love the direct approach of the Alaskans. They are not much for beating around the bush, or political correctness. They say it the way it is, and then get on with life. My smile faded quickly as we approached a steep down hill with a big drop-off on the outside. It got worse, a lot worse.

Brutus and Utah were in lead. I could count on Brutus. He was not only big enough but also would listen to me and control the team if things became ugly. This was a team that was capable of running too fast on the up-hills. When they hit down-hills, they were a dangerous team to drive, especially here with a heavily loaded sled and Peg lashed on top making a very unstable load. We were running in the Alaska Range. Anyone who knows anything about backcountry mountain trails can appreciate the kind of terrain we were trying to negotiate.

The dogs were speeding on the down-hills way too much. Brutus would help slow somewhat but even he wasn't that keen on following my, "easy" command. And, screaming, "EASY" with panic in your voice doesn't work. The sled was bouncing off trees and boulders. Peg's head was hanging off one side of the sled and I worried we might smash her head against a tree. The brake was only of limited use in the deep snow trench. Several times to provide enough drag I had to throw the sled on the side and hold on, dragging along behind over the stumps and rocks. I was being beaten half to death and was afraid we were going to destroy the sled. We crashed numerous times, once rolling down the steep mountain side to avoid crashing headlong into a tree. But the dogs were having fun!

The Happy River Steps were horrible. The final decent onto the Happy River was like jumping off a cliff. With no warning the entire team disappeared over the edge. Fifteen dogs, a fully loaded sled with one dog lashed on top, and me, bounced, tumbled, and slid to the bottom. The dogs were getting used to this and waited momentarily while I righted the sled and were off. The rest of the trail beyond into Rainy Pass was not much better. Beaten, battered, torn, and tired we got into Rainy Pass checkpoint after dark. Temp was 25 below with light snow. The rumor was a storm was brewing and likely to make Rainy Pass treacherous.

After tending the dogs I walked past the snow covered team to the leaders where Brutus was sleeping on the straw. I wanted to somehow thank him for helping me keep us together. Otherwise motionless his eyes opened when my headlamp beam fell on him. I patted his snow covered head gently and said, "Good dog, Brutus." He closed his eyes. I can't always tell what is going on in his furry head but I could tell he knew he had done exactly what he was born to do, and he knew he had done it very well. He also knew he would be doing it again in about 3 hours. I really admired his composure.

I wanted to be over Rainy Pass and the treeless saddle before the storm hit. Just after the pass was the Dalzell gorge. I planned my stay to make sure we made the Gorge in daylight. I slept fitfully for a couple of hours in the checkpoint worried about making the pass before the storm obliterated the trail or trapped us unprotected above the tree-line.

Dawn found us in a steady climb to the saddle. The snow was drifting and in the twilight the trail was almost impossible to see. We lost our way twice, but somehow thanks to Alto we managed to regain sight of the markers.

The wind was building but the scenery was spectacular. There were periods of blue sky and sunshine making the high tundra sparkle like a giant jewel. It was breathtaking. Then snow squalls would move through dropping visibility to about 50 feet reminding us that this can be dangerous country in storms. There were a couple of serious climbs but the dogs seemed to handle them with ease. I was impressed by those beautiful dogs. A whiteout completely obscured the view at the saddle but when we started to descend I knew we had passed it. Winds were 40 MPH but happily we were going down hill. Ahead we had to face the ominous Dalzell gorge before leveling out on the river before the Rohn checkpoint. I couldn't see much in the whiteout but I could feel the dogs picking up speed on the downhill. This was going to be a wild ride.

e-mail: Dear Jennifer, Hello my name is Jenifer or people call me Jeni. I'm a 6th grader at Marshall Elementary. The whole six grade students have to pick a musher and I picked Jim Warren, because he reminds me of my Aunts boy friend. See you later bye, Jenifer

Chris, March 9: What a day and it's not even over yet! I left for McGrath at 8:00 this morning. When we landed, we found a way to get to Nikolai, which is a little closer to the start. My Dad should be in here sometime tonight, but until then I am going to enjoy myself. The school/ community building that we are staying at has everything a wandering traveler might want. I haven't checked about showers, but there is hot food, high speed internet and power outlets to plug into. The people here are very friendly. Several young people have introduced themselves to me, and three even asked me for my autograph.

The best thing is that I finally got my cold weather. It was 35 below in McGrath this morning and it is 20 below here in Nikolai with a stiff wind. It is so cold that in 40 minutes I had created a coat of ice on my coat with my breath. Our pilot from McGrath to Nikolai, George Murphy, was extremely kind and seemed to be fairly competent at the stick (although I wouldn't really know, seeing as I'm not a pilot). I am comfortable wearing my jeans, a fleece coat, and a wind proof vest. Gloves and boots are mandatory, but since I don't have room to pack my boots, not wearing them is not an option. All my gear for two weeks, including poofy survival gear, is packed into two medium-sized duffels.

Dad is doing well. He is 2-3 hours behind schedule but is adjusting to safely run the Steps and Gorge in the daylight. He has all 16 dogs and is moving well. From what I hear, the Dalzell Gorge is pretty rough. Several teams have come in with broken sleds and battered bodies. One guy, I think it's Jim Lanier, broke-off several teeth.

Jim, Dalzell Gorge and Rohn: The Gorge was everything they have made it out to be. There were ice bridges past swirling water holes, trees and stumps trying to break you and the sled, steep down-hills into hairpin turns over ice bridges. For most of an hour my muscles were aching and screaming for relief. We crashed several times, sometimes intentionally to survive a hazard. We finally made it into Rohn, even more beaten and battered. I can never remember having more sore muscles; not sore from use, bruised and torn sore. Ahead on the next leg, 105 miles, we were to have the glacier to climb, buffalo tunnels, and the Farwell burn to contend with. I didn't rest well in Rohn apprehensive of what lay ahead.

It occurred to me you can drive dog teams in Michigan for 50 years and never learn much about driving a sled. The trails are just too good. But when you hit the Happy River steps, you are forced to learn a lot and learn it fast. The alternative is not pretty. In the 150 miles or so after Finger Lakes checkpoint I learned more about driving a sled than I ever thought possible. Fortunately, I did it without any broken bones or a broken sled. I was thankful.

Out of the Rohn checkpoint only a few hundred yards and running too fast, the dogs stepped just off the edge of the trail and onto the glare ice of a large river to find their bootied feet had no traction at all. A shrieking wind blew us sideways and we began to slide, accelerating away from the safety of the trail at an alarming speed. The ice sloped downward to open water and we were headed toward it. I frantically jumped on the carbide tipped sled brake with my full weight. No good! I grabbed one, then both, snow hooks and was pounding them into the ice. It hardly slowed us. We were in serious trouble. A strip of snow slowed us, almost stopped us, but the snow hook broke loose. A second strip of snow stopped our perilous slide.

Now what! I couldn't even stand on the ice in the wind. Thanks to Chris I had a pair of Yak Traks hanging on the sled. I put them on. Thanks Chris! I found that I could walk around ok, but when the wind gusts hit it still wasn't enough traction. The cold flowing rapids looked evil. The 15 scared and huddling dogs were in a knot and wouldn't move. The near vertical granite walls towering on all sides made it a natural wind tunnel. Snow was pelting us like a sandblaster. I stood on the narrow strip of snow that held us and pondered a way out. I couldn't see one. I worried the ice would break loose and we'd all float out into the swirling current. This was a picture of an artic hell. What to do? Should I walk away and save myself? No way!

I got the leaders untangled and tried to get them to pull the rest to safety. They were frozen with fear, except Brutus. Even he couldn't pull enough to make any headway. With Brutus scared but helping I found I could jerk the dogs about a foot at a time toward traction. Our only traction on the glare ice was the pair of Yak Traks on my feet. The risk was that if we all broke traction again I wasn't anywhere near the snow hooks. We wouldn't be able to hook down on the strip of snow. It had to work the first time. It was an ugly solution but it was all I had.

Working, sweating I tried to find the fine line between sliding downwind and pulling the team and sled toward the safety of the trail. We'd gain a little and sometimes lose much of it to the wind slamming into my back. Sometimes we only gained inches.

I know so few tunes this came as a surprise to me. For a couple of days I had this little tune playing in my head, "One day at a time sweet Jesus, that's all I'm asking from you." A surprise too was my muttering aloud when a gust of wind hit us and we lost 3 or 4 precious feet, "I'd just like a foot at a time, a reliable foot at a time, OK?" It was a tense time. I spent the next hour jerking the whole team and sled a foot or two at a time back to the trail.

Once off the river and on the trail the dogs were running hard to wear off their adrenalin from the river experience. We ran over a wolf-killed moose!! I couldn't believe it. It was like running over a small car! Then, on a downhill and moving fast, Ruby jumped on the opposite side of a small tree. There was a loud snap. She flipped into the air and came down on her back . She was on her feet instantly, shocked but ok. Her neck line broke, saving her life. Thank God for the wisdom to use breakable necklines.

The glacier was non-existent but there were sections of trail with no snow, just dirt and sharp jagged rocks sticking up through glare ice. It was impossible to control the sled. We slid sideways with no control and crashed into the sharp rocks slicing open my artic parka. Later, I camped that night with Jim Conner and several others at a wide spot in the trail called Buffalo Camp. It was cold and windy but I was very thankful when I zipped up the sleeping bag still warm and dry. Thankful too that the worst was behind us and we had come through it with little serious damage.

e-Mail: Hi Jennifer, My dad said you had some pictures you could send me, which would be terrific!

My 3rd class has been following Jim on the internet and we named our sled dog after your dog, Stormy. The children got all the names they could find in Jim's journal and they voted on the one they liked the best. Alto was a close second. We have been reading Chris' journal too and the children are really enjoying the whole experience. The children were wondering today if Stormy went to the Iditarod and what the names of the dogs in Jim's team were. If you get time, we'd love to know.

I have made an Iditarod display case in our school with things my dad lent me and we have Jim and Al's picture and biopic from iditarod.com in it too. The children moved a marker that represents Jim's team to Rohn today and were very excited about his progress. We have the checkpoints posted along the school walls. My daughter, Tara, who is in 4th grade at our school, shared an article about Jim that was in our Lansing paper with her class, so they also know about Jim too. I even had a boy in my class call me early in the morning because his mom was reading the paper and saw the article about a Michigan musher and he said "Yes, that's Jim Warren we're following him in the Iditarod." His mom was very impressed! My school email is below, and if I get the pictures there, I can pull them right up for the children in the classroom. I am reading Libby Riddles' Storm Run to the children and today, we also recorded the sunrise/sunset times for Barrow, Alaska for the past month. We are deep into Alaska and the Iditarod!

Let Jim and Chris know we are cheering them on from Haslett! Thanks for all your help! Zsuzsanna Mahon (Suzanna)

Stormy, Haslett School Favorite

Chris, March 9 Entry 2, Nikolai: Al Hardman came in at dinnertime tonight. He is really tired and really beat up. He has a bruise on his left hand and head and a scratch on his cheek from hitting a tree. He said he was seeing stars afterward. There are bruises all over his arms. His trip through the gorge and the Happy River Steps was apparently pretty rough. At one time, he went around a sharp corner and his foot was on the wrong runner. The long and short of it is that he went off the edge and flew 20 feet before landing upright. Even though he maintains that the Iditarod is a young man's game, and that he should stick to camping trips, he is still optimistic. He says the trail has been good overall and the dogs are doing great. The two dogs he dropped, Moose and Toby, are simply exhausted, and the rest of the team is eating and sleeping well.

We are waiting for early morning to bring my dad and Jim Conner in.

Jim, the Run into Nikolai: Running into Nikolai across lakes and swamps the dogs looked great. They were moving in sync like a machine. They were having fun and there was not a wasted motion. It was beautiful to see. This was the first time I had all the tugs hooked since the gorge about 150 miles back. I had been concerned they were too strong and fast to be safe. But just then I was enjoying all the power and speed they would deliver. This was the high point. I still had a large and strong team with the worst behind.

Entering Nikolai

Jim, Upbeat in Nikolai

I hadn't a clue that from here my struggle with the demons of fatigue and pain would crush my will to go on and nearly stop us. I would lose sight of Nome and the finish and barely have the will to go to the next checkpoint. My objectives would be reduced to seeing the next section of trail or getting past the next hill, or sometimes in desperation a much shorter objective. I think I sometimes left checkpoints out of habit or maybe shear stubbornness. Sometimes I become obsessed with finishing what I started.

Jim, Nikolai to McGrath: When leaving the Nikolai checkpoint, leader Brutus began limping badly so I stopped the team before we got out of the checkpoint. When I walked up to check him he looked away from me and held his legs rigid refusing to be checked. He relented when the vet arrived. We discovered a punctured wrist sack that had become infected. It was likely from a dog bite. I remembered he had a minor disagreement with Alto over a patch of straw to sleep on at Buffalo Camp.

As the vet led him away on a leash he didn't so much as glance at me or the team. You could read deep disappointment written all over him. I watched soberly as Brutus walked obediently with the vet around the end of the cabin to the dropped dog area.

I lost a big resource in Brutus. It was a real big downer. Brutus had kept the team together, me uninjured, and the sled in one piece, through the wild rides in the steps and gorge. I really missed the big ugly guy! In the heat of the afternoon I started to cycle leaders through lead position with very disappointing results. Only Alto and Utah were reliable.

While traveling at night across a series of swamps and lakes my headlamp went out. They do that. In a matter of minutes I burned out all my spare bulbs and my extra head lamp. I tried running in the dark since it was a bright night. It worked for a little while until we entered a thick spruce forest. It was really dark in the spruce, I couldn't see a thing. Then the trail turned sharply onto a river. I saw the crash coming and kicked violently to try to miss a tree and stump. I felt the searing pain of a hamstring pull. Apparently I didn't miss the tree. I regained my wits looking up at the stars thinking how beautiful they were. I was lying on my back in the snow down on the river. The sled had rolled down the slope and tangled the dogs. I had a sore head, my right leg had an obvious re-injured hamstring but everything else seemed ok. The trail was now running on the flat river ice so I went on in the dark. My head began really aching and my right eye was watering profusely so I decide to stop and light a driftwood fire and wait until daylight. I walked with my ax over to some drift wood on the river bank but before reaching it stepped off the edge of the solid ice. I spun around and slammed the axe into the solid ice behind and was able to climb up to solid footing. OK, I decided to stay by the sled until daylight! A half hour later a passing musher loaned me a headlamp so I continued toward McGrath hurting and confused.

My hamstring was re-injured, my head and eye were swollen and my next bulb was 30 miles up the trail in Takotna. I tried to evaluate my situation while running into McGrath. Tired, hungry, and hurting, I found it incredibly difficult to think; making tactical decisions was almost impossible. Into McGrath, I decided to do something about the tired and hungry and assess the situation when I awoke. I wasted 12 hours in McGrath trying to get my head together. I thought fatigue was messing with my thinking and didn't stop to consider a concussion. Finally, I decided to continue as planned and evaluate my situation on the run. I went to Takotna, 24 miles down the river, to do my mandatory 24 hour layover. I had bent but had not broken.

Chris, March 11: Chaos reigns when mushers are making decisions. This morning I received a message that my dad had re-injured his hamstring and was taking his 24 hour mandatory rest in McGrath, not Takotna as planned. I was naturally disappointed, not only because he was re-injured, but because he didn't make it to Takotna, which is where his supplies, and I, are located. I immediately began making plans to fly back to McGrath. After I made sure I had the toothbrush and clean underwear my dad had requested, I called and booked a flight for a body and Al Hardman's extra sled to McGrath. The ticket agent, hesitated for a moment, and asked if the body was alive. Apparently, they do have to ship corpses on occasion. On a whim, I then called the checkpoint in McGrath to check on Dad. When they put him on the phone, his first words were, "There is a change in plans. I'm coming to Takotna." Well that was inconvenient. I called the air service back, canceled the flight for me, but not the sled, and proceeded to wait for my dad to get in.

Jim Conner came in around 3:00 am this morning. He looks a ton more tired than he did in Nikolai. When he switched sleds in McGrath he was so tired he left his snowshoes on his old sled. About 3 miles out of the checkpoint, he realized his mistake, and had to turn his team around. "I had to take the team out of the checkpoint twice so they were real slow coming in." Jim has actually borrowed my dad's second sled. The only problem is that the new sled bag is much smaller than his original sled. He was rethinking his packing strategy when I last saw him. I have packed that sled myself and I will be amazed if he puts everything in the sled that he had sitting next to it. He has dropped Pluto, due to a wrist injury, and Only. He is enjoying his rest here in Takotna, but my guess is that he is enjoying the shower and delicious food even more.

Ed Stielstra has completed his 24 hour rest and is moving down the trail. I have heard about how banged up his leg is. Apparently it isn't too bad; he blew through Takotna today after rifling through his bags. His dogs looked good, according to Charlie, so I would imagine that he went to Ophir before resting.

"It would take a lot of money to go back and run that again," Dad said, "That and I'd have to be drunk." That statement over dinner effectively summarizes the 375 mile journey that my dad has already undergone. "The first couple days, whew, you need parachute practice," he said in between horror stories of catapulting down hills and careening off of trees. In addition to the typical terror of navigating the Steps and the Gorge, my dad also had a few close encounters. The first happened while he was traveling down a river. The leaders, Alto and Utah, tried to traverse an imaginary trail. Unfortunately they led the team onto glare ice. The dogs were instantly knotted up and, to make matters worse, there was an extremely strong wind accelerating the knotted team and the sled towards the open river. The brake and both snow hooks were enough to slow the team, but the wind was so strong that it forced the tangled mass of dogs and Jim towards the cold, dark water. The sled went over a section of packed snow where Jim was able to set the hook. However as he reached for the second hook, the wind ripped the first hook free. Then, miraculously, a second patch of snow was under the brakes. Jim quickly set both hooks. The team was secured, for now. Jim looked at the team and saw "a puddle of shivering, cowering, frightened dogs." "It looked like an artic picture of Hell," he said after describing the screaming wind and driven snow. After he drug the fear-frozen team 200 yards back to the trail, he started off again, down the river.

The second incident occurred the next night. He had burned out, or lost, all of his bulbs for his headlamp. As a result, he was driving the sled with a small chore lamp that only lets him see about 6 of 14 dogs. One particularly steep downhill had an acute turn at the bottom. Unfortunately Jim couldn't see the turn, and was braking hard. When he realized that there was a tree at the very corner of the turn, and that he was going to hit it, it was too late to do anything short of drastic. He gave a hard kick to get around the turn and felt a fiery stab in his injured leg. He doesn't know if he made it around the tree or not. The next thing he remembers is staring at the sky remarking at how pretty the stars and the northern lights were; then he realized he was supposed to be running a dog team. He looked around and found that the sled had rolled over and the dogs were waiting for him. After that he decided to build a fire and wait till morning.

Jim spied a piece of driftwood on the river bank and began walking towards it with an ax, intent on making some firewood. Halfway there, he stepped into open water with his left leg. As he fell into moving water of unknown depth, he spun around and slammed his ax into the ice. He was able to pull himself out and dry off but decided to wait on the sled for someone to come by. Eventually a fellow musher came by and gave him a spare headlamp that he could use. He ran the dogs the final 20 miles into McGrath wondering if he would be able to go on.

As I talked to him over a hamburger in Takotna, he said that he is "down, but not out." He had to drop one of his main leaders, Brutus, due to a dog bite on the wrist. He dropped Beta due to a bug and Dell due to dehydration. Four hours after he got in, the vets here had Dell on some drugs and an I.V to re-hydrate him.

My plan is to fly from here to Galena to Ruby and then to Unalakleet. If my dad stays to his plan, and rests the dogs and him excessively for a few days, then I think he will make it to Nome.

Resting 24 hours in Takotna

Jim, Takotna: In Takotna I had time to evaluate my plight. I was able to manage the leg pain with meds. But my injuries were greater than I had first thought. My hamstring was re-injured; a serious issue. My leg was of only limited use. I could walk OK on the level but where in Alaska is it level? It was going to be up to the dogs to pull me up the hills. Another disheartening surprise was I found my left hand was numb, no feeling, and I had blurred vision, obviously the result of a severe concussion. If I closed one eye the blurred vision was controlled. My numb hand made zippers and boot strings almost impossible but I could use the other hand in most situations. I worried my grip would be weak but it seemed ok when I tested it on the sled.

I bought extra bulbs for my headlamp from a musher who was scratching. I didn't say much, even to Chris, and tried to hide my condition because I feared the Iditarod officials might force me to scratch. I wasn't going to scratch voluntarily; it had to be that I absolutely with no doubt was not able to go on. We were heading for Nome!

Just before leaving Takotna I found I needed to drop another dog. That put the team at 11. Worse, I discovered it was very slow and difficult to bootie the dogs. I couldn't feel the booties with my left hand; I couldn't feel anything. But I left Takotna, rested, with some optimism. The dogs ran splendidly to Ophir. I dropped Ketchup there because she was still in heat and I didn't need more confusion in the shape I was in.

*e-**Mail:** Dear Jennifer: I know you are extremely busy, both on the internet and off, so I will be quick. While up in Tahquamenon for the race, Jim had shared his fear of re-injuring his hamstring and I'm so sorry to hear he has done so. Our prayers are with him and the dogs.*

Christopher is unbelievable. I have been following his web journal since the first day. The story about the wind and the ice was incredible. What a close call... Russ and I couldn't believe it!

We have been following your website and telling others to do so—a great source of information. Also, I can not begin to tell you how incredibly impressed I am with your son. You must be so proud.

Truly, the best coverage I have seen is through the eyes of Christopher.

Again, we are with Jim in both thought and prayer.

Sherry & Russ Sutherby, Mancelona, MI www. lastchancekennel.com

Chris, March 12: Well, enough about the mushers. Today we hopped on a chartered flight to Ruby, the first checkpoint on the Yukon River. The flight had been chartered by Aliy Zirkle's father and Randy Chappel's mother. We crammed into a 6 seated airplane. We had so much gear that I had to carry my parka and my computer bag on my lap. In addition to that, the plastic sleds that we use to transport our bags were wedged in between the seats on either side. The flight was beautiful. We were at 2100 feet when we started seeing dog teams. Then the pilot dropped the plane to 800 feet. He even maneuvered the plane so that Andy and Charlie could get some awesome pictures of both dog teams and the towns of Ophir and Ruby. For those of you who haven't been in Alaska and traveled by bush plane I have posted a picture of the mountains from the plane window. It truly is amazing to see the same type of thing as far as you can see in all directions. You all of a sudden feel really, really small. When we arrived in Ruby, we practically needed a pry bar to get out. I had to climb onto the wing on my hands and knees, and then get my stuff.

Chris Flying in Backseat of Bush Plane

Alaska from a Bush Plane

Once in Ruby, we had the opportunity to watch the top mushers head on out. The sleds that Martin Buser and Jeff King have, that allow the musher to sit down, are going to be big next year. Those guys looked well rested as they headed down the Yukon on their sleds. After we watched them go out, we caught a snowmobile ride up the hill to the school. It was interesting, riding the runners of an old freight sled being towed by a snowmobile. The sled riding skills I developed driving 16 dogs out of the yard came in handy. It would have really stunk to fall off of a sled at 30 mph on an ice road. After we arranged for a place to stay with the principal, my traveling companion Andy and I walked down to the checkpoint to see what was going on. We walked up to see Jeff King getting ready to leave after his 24 hour mandatory break. After his excellent looking team blasted on out of the checkpoint, Andy and I tried to find some food. We were pointed to a house where we could ask a knowledgeable person and started walking.

When we got to the house, the host for the Outdoor

Channel's coverage of the Iditarod was leaving with a truckload of people. As we walked up the stairs to introduce ourselves to the lady who lived there, she said "My name is Florence, be with you in moment," like an auctioneer on caffeine. After she finished her chore, we told her our situation, and she insisted that we come in. It seems that the Outdoor Channel people had just left her with a full dinner prepared and only a few people to eat it. She welcomed us to have our fill of a delicious chicken noodle soup and spaghetti. That spaghetti was the best thing I have had in, literally, months. She couldn't remember exactly what she had put in, but there was moose burger, Jimmy Dean's spicy sausage and a few other ingredients in the sauce. Because it was my only meal today, I had a large plate of spaghetti, a bowl of homemade chicken noodle soup, an apple, and best of all, pineapple upside down cake. The only bad thing about the meal was that there was too much food and I didn't have enough stomach.

After dinner we started walking back up to the school. It is about a half mile up a 5 % grade. We caught a ride halfway up, fortunately. The unfortunate part was that I was stripped down to my unzipped fleece jacket. The spray of snow from the snow machine covered me in white, packed snow. So now I am here in the school drying off and getting ready for bed.

Chris, March 13 and 14: Al Hardman left Ruby today. He looks like a typical Iditarod musher with a swollen face and hands from near constant exposure to cold, a vacant stare when he tries to think. Long pauses before speaking, and wasted motions are common. He is glad to get on the Yukon; it means shorter runs and flatter trail. These in turn translate to better rested dogs. He plans to do something at the coast,"We got a secret plan. We don't know what it is, but we'll get it formulated when we get there."

I managed to talk to Ed Stielstra today. He looks a far sight better than Al, except for his leg. Based on the descriptions I have heard, it sounds like he may have a hairline crack of his femur. Very painful, but the amount of swelling and bruising that I have seen is consistent with what I have seen in other fractures and breaks. The good thing is that the swelling is going down, and that he is able to walk without limping too badly. He is feeling good enough to be competitive, but he is too dazed with fatigue to figure out what to compete for.

On a side note, just about everyone I meet wants to know when I am going to run this crazy race. You only need to read the last couple entries I have made to realize why I am hesitant about doing it. Even Ed, with his injured leg, said I should do it. His advice is to find someone to beat the hell out of you with a hockey stick, that way you know what to expect.

I'm getting a little worried about my dad. He has been spending way too long at checkpoints; I hope that the ITC won't ask him to quit due to his lag time from the leaders. He only has 10 dogs and has spent almost 12 hours in Cripple. He hasn't been leaving me messages, so I can only assume that he is ok, and that the dogs are slow due to a bug or warm weather.

The trip is still interesting for me. We caught a ride to Galena today, 50 miles downriver from Ruby. We found floor space again tonight, this time for free. The food here is good, but the restaurant closes at eight, presumably to protect the patrons from being harassed by the people at the bar who increase exponentially at eight o'clock. There is no high speed connection here at our lodging but there is one for media people at the checkpoint. I am getting impatient for news on my dad. Thank goodness I have press credentials.

Jim, Ophir, to Cripple, to Ruby: Pressing on into Cripple then Ruby became a struggle of near epic proportion. The next 30 hours and 150 miles, finally into the Ruby checkpoint was the lowest point I've ever experienced. The dogs came down with major intestinal illness, weather was hot, trail was filled with moguls, I was in agony but still trying to run the team, and I had no more pain meds. I camped for a 4 hour rest at the point I had calculated to be 45 miles before Cripple.

Alone in the dark sitting on my cooler, hurting too much to get up and spread out the sleeping bag, I dug into my food bag for a dose of calories to keep me warm while I slept on top on the sled. Daughter Whitney had slipped little notes of encouragement into my food bags. I picked one out of the bag really needing a lift. To my utter dismay I discovered my blurred vision had worsened to the point I couldn't read the note. I knew enough about closed head injuries as a Fire Department Medical First Responder to know I had been taking a big risk. Closed head injuries can and do result in permanent brain damage and death. I had been taking large amounts of Aspirin and Advil since the borrowed pain meds had run out. Aspirin tends to make you bleed more easily. The worsened vision was a clear sign the injury had progressed. There was no way to predict how this was going to turn out.

I was mentally crushed, beaten, and knew I'd never make it to Nome! This was a very difficult time. Alone in my sleeping bag on a dogsled in the Alaskan wilderness, I faced myself in a way I had never done.

Death has never been something I have feared. As a car racer and as a firefighter I had often been graphically reminded of my own mortality. This was a little different. Death from a brain hemorrhage seemed almost a good alternative to the agony of defeat that I was experiencing. It fell on me like an avalanche and swept me along an emotional rollercoaster. At first I was simply heartbroken and indulged in tons of self pity. But quickly I became very angry and defiant.

My memory took me back to a point in my life where I got great support from a poster I kept in my office. It was of a little mouse backed into a corner watching in horror as a vicious eagle streaked down at him with talons ready for the kill. The little mouse had enough fire left in his soul to shake his fist at the eagle. I hadn't thought of that poster for years. But that night I again saw myself as the little mouse. I still had enough fire to fight back.

With a little mouse as my role model, I thought through revised race plan. It was interrupted by coyotes making a big ruckus up the trail. The moon was dark but the northern lights were bright enough for me to see a canine shadow stealthily circle the dog team and me. It moved away.

My plan was simple. If I awakened, we would move on. Nome was no longer in the picture, just the next checkpoint. One checkpoint at a time, maybe one hill at a time, was as large a view as I could handle. As long as I could still walk and hold my head up we were going to keep moving. I had bent, and broken. But we were not out! I struggled to find reasons to keep on going.

Alone in the dark resting in my sleeping bag on the sled I could hear the dog's stomachs growling. When time came to feed and get ready to go I found they were definitely very sick and not thrilled about running. I thought if I got them into Cripple I could nurse them through the illness with the help of the vets. The run into Cripple was sunny and too warm, the trail filled with moguls, and there were bone jarring creek crossings that were to numerous to count. I was having a lot of trouble handling the sled and it was wearing on the already sick dogs. Time wore on and I worried I'd missed the turn to Cripple. We had been warned about missing that turn-off in the Rookies Meeting. Finally, sure I'd missed the turn, I stopped the team for a 4 hour rest during the heat of the day. I didn't know whether to go on or turn back to look for the turn. How could I have missed it in the daylight! Perhaps a more experienced Musher would come by who knew. Reluctant to turn back, as the sun started to descend we started ahead. To my delight and dismay we arrived at the Iditarod Checkpoint of Cripple in about 15 minutes!

With meds from the vet I medicated the dogs. On his advice I planned to stay about 12 hours or as long as needed to be sure all dogs were eating and drinking. It was the best way to know they were on the mend and to keep from having to haul several dogs at once in the sled. I slept well in the Alaskan wall tent at the checkpoint. I had put the agony of defeat behind me and had a new race plan.

Cripple to Ruby was nearly a disaster. I couldn't read my run sheet anymore so had to rely on memory or others advice. The distance was said to be about 65 miles and trail was to be better than what we'd just come off. Run time was told to be 7 or 8 hours worst case. Because of my worsened eyesight which I presumed was a result of my head injury I had stopped taking anything to manage the leg pain that may cause bleeding. It seemed the damaged muscle was now trying to spasm and sometimes would go into an outright cramp. I struggled for mile after mile. The dogs were sick. The trail was not too bad; but frankly I don't really remember much about it. But nobody will ever convince me it was only 65 miles. It took us 14 hours to get to Ruby! Without exaggeration, that was the longest 14 hours of my life.

Somewhere before Ruby we had to traverse about ¼ mile of overflow. It was a glaciered area where the trail was covered with a sloping sheet of ice from springs on the uphill side. It was 'side-hilling' at its best or maybe worst. The side-hilling configuration is to tip the sled up on the uphill runner and balance it, standing on the runner with one foot and using the other foot to occasionally push the sled back up to keep the balance. Think of wrenching a 250 Lb sled up on one runner, holding it there with one arm while the dogs pick their way across slippery and rough slanted surfaces. Well, with a pulled hamstring this was agony. I'd rather take a whipping than do that again.

Shortly after the side-hill, I had to stop the team to work the cramps out of my leg. I could not go on. I bent over the sled handlebar to stretch the muscle. I mentally quit, that was it, I couldn't go another foot. I looked up to tell someone, "I quit!" But there was nobody there! I looked up the trail, back down the trail, then across the miles of rolling hills to see no-one, nothing, not even a recent track. There was nobody within miles. I thought, "You can't quit if there is nobody to tell!"

As I think back on that incident, I am embarrassed. Let there be no doubt, whatever physical and mental toughness I thought I had wasn't enough. I offer no excuses; I was past my limit. The Iditarod Trail had humbled me. Fortunately, I didn't quit because I couldn't. I went on.

Not obvious to me at the time was my significant calorie deprivation. Only a small part of my food was useable. The extent of this problem was never obvious to me during the race. I was really never hungry. But my body including my brain was under extreme stress. It made the sick dogs and hurting musher seem even worse.

Into the Iditarod Checkpoint of Ruby, exhausted, hurting, sick dogs and out of anything resembling the will to go on, I knew I had to sleep before I considered my options. I fed, bedded, and med'ed the dogs and then after the vet check I stumbled into the checkpoint building. The other mushers sensing my state began to probe and then offer encouragement. The biggest encouragement was that Galena, 50 miles downstream on the flat Yukon River, was a much better place to fly out of if one were to scratch. Another thought was the dogs would heal if given the easy runs on the Yukon.

My rest in the checkpoint was interrupted several times with leg cramps. I think this was somewhat entertaining to checkpoint workers but definitely an annoyance to other tired mushers. Finally I did get some sleep. Somehow after resting for a couple of hours, I awakened. I could still walk, and hold up my head. I don't even remember thinking about it, I went on. I don't remember prepping the team to leave but I did. Apparently I aimed the dogs at the big river, began following the trail markers, and just kept going.

My first conscious memory was the gut-wrenching fear of not knowing where I was. I could see I was following Iditarod Trail markers on a wide flat river; the mother of all rivers judging by the width of it. I turned over my left shoulder and saw a rock promontory with a village on the hillside behind the rock. I struggled to remember coming down a hill in the dark into Ruby. So, I reasoned, that the village was Ruby; it better be Ruby! Then I almost panicked wondering if I was going the right direction. Slowly I reasoned if I came down the hill in the dark then following the markers on the river had to be the right direction. Still worried, I checked inside the sled bag while moving to be sure I had supplies like dog food. I noticed Hartley was bulging just behind his rib cage indicating he had just eaten. Somehow, with no conscious memory I was back on the trail. Fortunately, my relentless pre-race practice of the checkpoint routine had served me well. I had, like a robot without conscious thought, prepped the team and left the Iditarod checkpoint of Ruby.

The flat Yukon River was without wind and the clouds kept the temperature down. I remember sitting on the sled seat with my arms through the handle bar and a rope tied to my wrist. In case I dozed off I didn't want to fall off the sled and loose my team. I don't remember much else about this 50 mile run. I didn't know at the time that the dogs and I were 'healing while running'. It would make the critical difference days later in the long steep climbs in the hills along the sea coast.

e-Mail: Hi Jennifer- If you talk with Jim today please let him know I am thinking about him and his team. I have read Chris' reports along the trail. I have been watching everyone's progress. Sitting here in a nice warm classroom it is easy to talk but with the very deepest concerns I wish him the strength to run and rest the dogs and nurse them to Nome if at all possible. What a beautiful sight to see that burled arch! From personal experience of marathon canoe racing I know how hard it may seem but it is worth everything to finish. Tell him all of my LOUD second graders are cheering him along. We're proud of him. Cheers to you also back home wishing the best for Jim and his team. Lynne.

Chris, March 14: Well today was another long wait. I

sincerely hope my Dad and my dogs are OK. They have really slowed. With not many choices, I wandered around the checkpoint (Galena) for awhile, and basically killed time and got the lay of the land. During my wanderings I learned, much to my dismay, that the people in the checkpoint were claiming the leftover food from the mushers left behind bags. You see, I have been able to glean a meal or so a day from the excess food. It is very excellent and almost always vacuum packed.

So faced with the prospect of shelling out 15 dollars for a meal, or going hungry (oh no!!!), I decided to become a volunteer. Around 3:30, I walked to the checkpoint and started scooping poop. Then I talked to the checkpoint coordinator and received instructions for picking up dog straw. So, after two and a half hours of picking up straw with a fellow Michiganian, Dale Peterson, I signed, the official volunteer sheet and had a meal. It really is amazing to talk to the people here. Most of them are very congenial and almost all are willing to swap stories.

The typical check point seems to be filled with a three types of people. Mushers are all bleary eyed and concerned with the trail ahead. They occasionally get talking about horror stories of the trail behind them, but it all merges to one question: What's next? The next category is the organizers/pilots. That group is constantly working, and reworking, logistics. That and they are nearly constantly comparing notes on the weather and who is flying where. They have to, everything changes so quickly. The third group in the checkpoints is the resting workers. This is the best group for entertainment. As with any group of people stuck together with good food and excessive time on their hands, the jokes, stories, and time killers fly. I heard a few bad ones, a few good ones, a few great ones, and more than a couple I don't dare repeat.

Jim Conner just left a few minutes ago. He is looking refreshed, and his dog team took off like a train, smooth, powerful, and accelerating to an efficient pace. He is somewhat concerned about only having 9 dogs left, but as he said, "What can I do, they aren't coming back soon." He was thrilled with the hospitality here at Galena. In my opinion, the crew here at Galena should give a clinic on how to treat mushers. The water, straw, and drop bags were at Jim's sled minutes after he set the hook.

The more I become involved in this race, the more I see, hear, and observe the more I think that I will be coming back here. I don't know when, or how, but I have a gut feeling that my experiences on this trip will leave me wanting more. I know that I have changed as a person since I left home on the 18th of February, simply because home is no longer located in Linwood, Michigan. It's not even in the same state. Home has become a concept, rather than a place. Home is now wherever I feel at ease, both in body and soul. I know I feel that way in Montana, Alaska, and Michigan's Upper Peninsula. This small office is home for the few days I have spent here. I know my mom won't like it too much, but I think that the days of coming home to stay are gone. I may come to visit, but the only thing worth staying for at the Christmas tree farm and the white house where I grew up is the people. I love my family dearly, but they are no longer the center of my life and focus of my energies. My parents must have done a good job raising me. I am ready to leave the nest, so to speak, but I don't need to escape. It is simply time to begin a new chapter in my life.

e-Mail: Dear Jennifer: We have been reading Chris' web journal entries and have found them quite interesting. I just thought you might need a good pat on the back and perhaps some moral support after reading his entry about 'home'! A job well done, I'd say! What more could a mother ask? Mary Eleanor and Kenny

Chris, March 15: Today is not a good day. I talked to Dad on the phone. He is down to one real leader, Alto, and the dogs are nearly beat. The team has several minor dings, and he is questioning his ability to manage the long, hard hills along the coast. His leg is next to useless, and his inability to manage the sled is wearing on the dogs. He is contemplating scratching in either Galena or Unalakleet. He is thinking of what his options are, and seems really down. He needs all the prayers he can get. My sense is that he is beaten mentally, not physically. I sincerely hope that he will make it to Unalakleet, where I am waiting.

Off the Yukon River into Galena at Dusk

Jim, Galena: In the Iditarod Checkpoint of Galena, more dead than alive, I learned Chris had been there and had gained a great deal of respect from the checkpoint folks. That one comment seemed to lift my spirits. They had some good chow! I don't remember what it was but it was very good! I awoke before my planned time and left in the dark. Food seemed to make a big difference! But I was taking forever to get the dogs bootied because of the numbness in my left hand. I worried about getting frostbite too.

Chris, March 16: I woke up at 3:00 am last night. I was going to call my dad back at Galena to give him some encouragement. When I called the checkpoint, he was already outside, putting booties on the dogs, getting ready to leave. I am glad that he has decided to press on. He has several miles of easy river to go; the dogs will enjoy it. I hope that I can get a hold of him before he gets here in Unalakleet. He tends to over think things when he is alert, and he can't think clearly at all when he is tired. I need to talk to him and assess his dog team. Until then, he doesn't have a justifiable reason to quit, unless something catastrophic happens.

Jim, From the Yukon River to the Sea Coast: Into Nulato, I was thinking I'd finish the three Yukon runs and scratch upon arriving in the final Yukon River checkpoint, Kaltag. I dreaded the climb after Kaltag at the beginning of the 90 mile overland trip to Unalakleet on the coast. Before the race my doctor warned me not to continue should I re-injure my hamstring. He said, "I don't want you getting killed trying to race the Iditarod with one leg."

I was caught in a vise, an unsolvable condition. I was convinced, sure at a gut level, that we would not make it up the big hills along the coast of Norton Sound. The hamstring re-injury of my right leg felt like someone was jamming a screwdriver into it when I had to use it. On the hard climbs I was unable to do much to help the dogs. I expected they would balk, just quit, sit down and refuse to go, on the side of some hill with a 30 below wind shrieking up our backs. I couldn't blame them. Although normally optimistic, I couldn't shake this ominous picture.

On the other side, my overdeveloped personal drive pushed me on. There was nothing in me, not a fiber in my body, that would let me quit voluntarily. No way! I've lived my life holding to the standard: If I can still hold up my head, if I can still walk, then keep moving.... to work, to school, whatever. Perhaps somewhat harsh, it has served me well. But then it was part of a power play in my fatigued brain.

Now, there is a lot of time on the trail for the musher to think, a word used loosely under the conditions. I was on one side and then on the other side of the issue. Finally, recognizing that no resolution would ever come, I determined it would have to be, not my decision, but something, an event, that would end our race. It could be the finish line in Nome but I thought that was unlikely. It may be a storm, a dogfight injuring my leaders, or simply a team balk, stopping, refusing to move. I didn't try to find the event, just the opposite. I worked like a demon to manage around anything that might be the "event." We were moving from objective to objective, one checkpoint at a time, one hill at a time, and sometimes in desperation, a much, much shorter objective. Step by step, hour by hour, mile by mile and day by day, we were moving ahead.

Filled with apprehension I tended the dogs in the dark behind a building in the Iditarod checkpoint of Kaltag. After days of running on the Yukon River I was facing a critical obstacle, the climb out of Kaltag on the portage trail to sea coast village of Unalakleet. I was very apprehensive, paranoid with the fear I would not be able to make the climb.

A bearded fellow with a big camera, who had helped me park the dogs when I arrived, returned with a pep talk. He said, "I've handled a lot of dogs, and yours are strong. They will go the distance to Nome easily." He was full of encouragement. He logically pointed out all the positive things I had going for me then warned me not to be my own worst enemy. The epitome of positive thinking, he reminded me of my favorite TV pastor, Dr. Robert Schuler of the Hour of Power. He knew how to capture the attention of the trail weary musher. He stood directly in front of me when he spoke, about two feet from my face. I was giving him my full attention, almost hypnotized. He was a good, kind man.

Now, how could he have spoken so precisely to my paranoia? I hadn't told anyone about some of the things he touched on. It was as if he was reading my mind. This was a curious encounter.

Somehow, I found myself out of Kaltag on the 90 mile trail to Unalakleet. The dogs pulled me up the hill and I was feeling better than I had for some time. But as I thought of the trail ahead, the artic coast was an ominous place. Then there were the steep hills, like The Blueberry Hills, Little McKinley, and Topkok. I was sure my re-injured leg would never handle the big hills. I was so depressed and so very, very tired of hurting. But I noticed I was trying to find reasons to go to the next checkpoint.

We camped at Old Woman, a BLM shelter cabin about 40 miles before Unalakleet. The temperature was dropping and the gusty wind was whipping up the snow. The run through the open country ahead into Unalakleet was going to be tough.

Alone, in the cabin I found left over food from other mushers. Like a starving animal I began stuffing my mouth with both hands until the food was falling all over the floor. I wasn't embarrassed; I was desperate.

After a couple hours of sleep I noticed the banging from the wind on the outside of the cabin had stopped. When I stepped outside to check on my dogs I found the wind nearly calm. I felt a surge of encouragement for the first time in days. The 40 mile run into Unalakleet was cold but pleasant.

e-Mail: Hi Jennifer, It's me again, Sherry/Russ from Last Chance Kennel.

I see Jim is resting in Kaltag (according to the latest updates). At least he is getting off the Yukon—a mental sign for him that things are moving forward.

He is in Russ and my prayers, day and night. I will also add him to the prayer list at our local church.

I was in the kennel late last night and flipped off my headlamp and just stared at the stars, trying to imagine what it is like for the mushers...seeing those same stars under very different conditions. Amazing and overwhelming.

I can only imagine what limits are being pushed; physically and mentally. I'm sure it helps Jim to know that Chris is there, one jump ahead. It's too bad that Andy and Charlie have to leave checkpoints before Jim arrives, but I'm sure it will work out for Chris. (That kid lands on his feet.) And, by the small sampling of Jim's writing, his passion for his family must be a constant source of strength. I hope we get to see more of his writing once the race is over.

As for Chris, I used to be an Assistant Editor of a local 4-color glossy magazine and I can tell you, Chris' writing has made me laugh, tear up and gasp. This young man has a bright future, as you must know. Obviously his school knew, since I see he was top of his class, and awarded for his hard work. Take care and God Bless, Sherry

Unalakleet from the Air with Open Sea Beyond the Ice Shelf

e-Mail: Hi Jennifer, I have no idea where you are or if you'll even have access to this, but I decided to try anyhow. Following this race on the internet has become excruciating! Cabela's and Iditarod are not posting updates nearly so often now that all the big guns are in ... shame on them with so many still on the trail!

Anyhow, I've no idea if weather, sick dogs, battered mushers or communication breakdowns are delaying mushers and info. Al has been resting way more than usual, and Conner (with 2 others) has been on the trail for 20 hours on what should be a 7-8 hour run from Shaktoolik to Koyuk. I worry about these guys! If you can find out what's up, please send me some info.

It's good to see that Jim decided to continue ... his time/speed between checkpoints seems to be pretty good! Traveling in the pack with Bennie and Sue Allen should help keep his spirits up as well.

Thanks for any help from your end. Katie

e-Mail: Hi! I am a teacher at Bangor West Elementary and we are studying the Iditarod and have for a few years! We include all the students in the activities and this fall the classes walked 1049 miles to Nome for fitness!

We have been following Jim Warren for the race and the kids are sure interested. I was reading the web journal of Chris and it sounds like Jim is getting frustrated and discouraged! Tell him that there are 300 students from Bangor West cheering him on daily and asking what checkpoint he is at! We hope to get him to talk to us when he gets back to Michigan! The kids think he should go for the Red Lantern Award! At our school "musher banquet" that was one of the favorite prizes! So tell him from these students and teachers to hang in there and follow Martin Buser's advice and to not quit 'til he's talked to 3 people (one of the being Martin!) My sister is friends with Martin and Kathy Buser in Alaska -she lives in Wasilla-so if Chris ever needs anything tell him to call the Koutskys!

Anyhow, Good luck, get rest and tell Jim to press on! If it's in their best interest and even if he does scratch-he has done something truly amazing and something that most of us only dream of doing! -That is not failure!

Our prayers are with you and your family! Hope to see you in Michigan at Bangor West Sometime. Mush! Shelly Smith

Jim, Unalakleet: In Unalakleet, down on the river ice in the dark of the checkpoint a big shadow walked over to me and excitedly shouted, "Mr. Warren," and then bear-hugged me, pulling my feet off the ground. The voice sounded strangely familiar through the mental fog of fatigue but I couldn't identify the person. Then it hit me; it was Chris! What a boost. I told him my food was not working and I wanted him to order pizza, lots of it! He looked at me like I was crazy. I told him I knew the pizza guy and he would make pizza anytime. Still skeptical, he agreed to try. He called from the checkpoint and got the only pizza man for 300 miles out of bed at midnight and ordered enough pizza for the whole checkpoint. I had found the reason to go to the next checkpoint! I stuffed the sled full of leftover pizza. My stomach was full for the first time in over a week. The dogs were feeling better. Dawn was breaking when I left the checkpoint and the dogs were barking and jumping, impatient to be off. We were running in convoy with Ben Stamm and Sue Allen. A convoy was much better.

Chris, March 18: Whew, disaster averted! It turns out that my dad had hit what veteran mushers call "the wall." He was so tired that he couldn't do anything but think of reasons to quit. I managed to talk him into coming to Unalakleet with the idea of talking to him there. The thing was he was smiling when he got here. He had teamed up with Sue Allen and Ben Stamm and has been convoying with them since the Yukon River. I talked with him and then ordered pizza for us. Several mushers wanted some food so I wound up spending $120 on pizza. The mushers paid me back, but the owner of the pizzeria was glad to get up at 12:30 am to make the food. To be truly honest I have never seen my dad eat so much. He devoured all of a large pizza, in addition to a big brownie and three cookies. After that he laid back on the floor and instantly fell asleep in the warm checkpoint building. My dad and I both want to express our sincere thanks for all the support we have received. We wouldn't be here without it.

By the time we finished eating it was 2:30 in the morning. Rather than go back to the house I was staying at, I decided to sleep at the checkpoint. When I woke up at 5:00 my dad was still sleeping. He wanted to be up at 5:00, but was lifeless except for the sound of his breathing. Still lying on the floor, I kicked his feet gently a couple times. He didn't budge. I kicked him again, a little harder this time, and he mumbled something about sleeping all the way to Nome. After a few more tries at waking him I gave up and sat at the table, sipping my coffee. He soon got moving. When he finally pulled the hook to leave the checkpoint, the dogs were barking in harness, ready to go, and a golden sunrise was giving birth to a gorgeous day.

Shortly after my dad left, I hopped on a plane bound for Nome. Now in Nome, it feels strange being at the endpoint of this journey, just waiting for it to end. I will have to find a way to meet my Mom somewhere. She came up to see Dad finish, and then explore this town a little more. Nome is a lot larger and a big change from the towns in the bush that I have been staying in.

I apologize for not responding to emails. In the past two days I have received in excess of 100 messages from people who wish my dad encouragement. Responses are coming, but they may take awhile.

e-Mail: Hi Jennifer, Position 73 (up one) and 261 miles to go. Not to mention, he is in good company.

If the dogs are willing, I hope Jim can endure the pain of his leg and trudge on. It has to be grueling. I also hope the wind dies down—the dogs don't need to be pushing through drifts, nor does Jim need to be slammed around on the sled by the wind. It sounds like he has done enough of that already.

That is awesome that you are in Nome. I don't know when you will have a link up to get this, but please know that I called the church and people are praying for Jim, his leaders and the rest of the team.

Prayers coming your way...Now enjoy Nome and all the glory of this great race!!!!!
Sherry

Jim, Unalakleet to Shaktoolik: The Blueberry Hills were horrible. I was mad at myself for even trying. The leg hurt a lot but somehow seemed to be feeling a little better, the dogs stronger. I wondered if it was real or if I was so far gone I was imagining it. It was real. I thought if I can just make it to Shaktoolik, the next two legs were quite flat. Good. Nome? Maybe?

Jim, Shaktoolik to Koyuk: The run across the Norton Sound to Koyuk was flat; miles upon miles of sea ice. The temperature was below minus 30 and there was wind and some drifting and it was at night. This was a cold run!

There is something ominous about facing the 50 mile crossing of open sea ice as you leave the tiny treeless spit that holds Shaktoolik. Every nerve in your body tightens. The dogs feel it too and are uneasy. This is for real. There is no 911 rescue team to call if things go wrong. You instinctively reassure your leaders and begin peering into the darkness, searching for the first view of the lights of Koyuk. Nothing matters but getting there, nothing matters.

At one point I noticed a set of polar bear tracks. They were days old but a reminder that this was their country, we were just visitors. I pulled off my artic mitts and reached inside the sled bag to check on the location of the .44 Mag revolver that I carried. The cold heavy steel object felt comforting. It is unlikely to have a confrontation with a bear but I was ready for the unlikely. My dogs were not going to be a lunch for Mr. Bear!

Jim, Koyuk to Elim: Finally, into the checkpoint of Elim, just for a moment I let myself think that Nome was possible; not likely but possible. I had been keeping my focus on one checkpoint at a time; sometimes one hill at a time was all I could handle. I couldn't bring myself to think about what lie ahead. But to get to Nome, Little McKinley had to be gotten over between Elim and White Mountain. Then out of White Mountain were Topkok and the Blow Hole. I dreaded the big hills (In Michigan these are mountains) and thought I could never make it. But I was elated to remember there was only one more checkpoint, White Mountain. We had come over so much, could I let the big hills stop us?

Jim, Elim to White Mountain: Pressing On Regardless! I awoke from a short rest in the checkpoint, pulled on my boots and parka and prepared the team to leave in the dark. Damn it, I was going to see just how tall this mountain really was! I left Elim. The dogs ran down onto the jumbled sea ice and took off like idiots. They were running too fast but it was fun! I began to sweat driving the sled. My leg began hurting a lot but I never thought it would be because the dogs were running too fast on the rough sea ice. There were frozen blocks of ice a large as houses. The dogs hit the first grade of Little McKinley and didn't break stride. They pulled me most of the way up. I was elated. I had to run the last few hundred yards and remembered painfully why I dreaded the big hills. I made it, sweating, hurting, but happy! I was very thankful to those beautiful dogs who hauled me up the mountain. A ray of sunlight hit me as we crested Little McKinley. As I looked over my shoulder at the stunning sunrise across the artic mountain landscape, I believed it was there just for me. I had paid a big price for the luxury of viewing that sunrise, but I didn't stop the team to take a long look. I had White Mountain checkpoint in the crosshairs.

The route took us through the small town of Golovin. I anticipated a problem. I thought the dogs would be let down if we didn't stop for some warm chow and rest in the straw. So I stopped on the sea ice and gave them snacks a mile or so out of Golovin hoping it would boost their motivation long enough to get us past. The problem was the trail leaves Golovin, again on the ice, a flat, straight as an arrow run for 17 miles to White Mountain. You can see Golovin for an hour after leaving. After Golovin they started looking back first at the town, then at me. The message was clear, "Hey You! You missed the checkpoint! It is back there!" The team was on the edge of a balk! This would be very bad at this stage. Getting them going again would be very unlikely.

Before the balk developed, I snacked again with the best I had. I massaged the leaders a little, and switched Utah for Reba. I hoped it would make Utah mad; anything to change the subject and get their furry little heads off of the town in sight behind. It worked, kind of. We moved ahead slowly for a mile or two. I tried switching leaders, moving around team dogs, putting dogs in heat in a more forward position, anything and everything I could think of. It worked. We were moving very slowly but we were moving. Once Golovin was out of sight, they picked up their normal speed. Whew, crisis weathered.

Jim, White Mountain to Nome: At the White Mountain checkpoint we had 77 miles to go into Nome. It seemed like a very long way! My leaders were tired and crabby and were fighting with each other. If anything happened to them we were stopped. I decided to run them each in single lead so they wouldn't fight. On my mind was Topkok, a notoriously steep set of hills, and on the far side the Blow Hole, a killer. But, the weather was the best it had been for days. Even before resting, I made the decision to go for it and take what came. After sleeping an hour or so I pulled on my parka and boots and headed out to care for the dogs. My paranoia was alive and well. I dreaded leaving the checkpoint in the gathering dusk. But I noticed I bootied the dogs faster than I had for days. I had learned to bootie faster without feeling in my left hand.

The Village of White Mountain

Unbelievable! The leaders had been to Nome and seemed to know they were getting near the end. They fired up a dog team that had over 1000 miles on them. They were to need all the fire they could muster. The steepness of Topkok was horrible. Repeatedly I had to push the sled behind the dogs, sometimes 50 or 100 feet at a time before resting. On some of the down-hills I could see in my headlamp what I thought was the canyon wall directly ahead. To my dismay it was the uphill trail directly ahead and oh so steep. It was good it was at night so I couldn't see too much of the steepness of the trail ahead. Through the darkness we pushed on.

So absorbed by my own physical struggle with the leg pain I hadn't noticed until then. The dogs without command were pulling like demons on the steep up-hills. I noticed in my headlamp on one particularly steep section that they were to a dog straining so hard their bellies were almost on the snow. I was so overwhelmed I had tears in my eyes. It seemed they knew how I was struggling and were doing all they could to take care of me. I marveled and thanked them profusely. I wished I could be as tough as the dogs but then wondered if some of them were hurting too. How would you tell?

Finally we dropped off Topkok and down on the flat we passed the USFS shelter cabin at the beginning of the Blow Hole. The wind was calm. We hurried ahead in the night to capture this gift, a wonderful window of calm winds.

We arrived at Safety, 22 miles out of Nome in what seemed almost record time. My dogs knew we were getting close and were barking and jumping in harness while I checked in with the officials. Finally my optimism and confidence returned.

Jim: Thin Ice: The lights of Nome were in the distance. We dropped off the beach when I noticed the dual trail markings and was confused. It looked like it was marked in two directions. Before I could confirm the dogs took the straight ahead route down on some very smooth ice. The ice was black and appeared to have frozen very recently. As I looked around, alarmed, a series of cracking sounds petrified both me and the team. I yelled, "Whoa" just as the leaders moved out on some even blacker ice. The cracking sounds continued and I felt the ice sag. I had to move fast. I yelled, "Haw," noticing the harder ice about 50 yards to our left. Just as the leaders started to move left the ice gave away beneath them. Panic struck the entire team as they lunged left pulling the frantic leaders backward out of the water onto the firmer ice. Slipping and sliding the team pulled me across the treacherous cracking ice to safety. I turned them back to the fork in the trail to warn Ben Stamm coming behind. My newly regained confidence and optimism had vanished. Waiting for Ben I had a talk with the team. It went something like this, "Ok you guys! We've come 1100 miles. Over there are the lights of Nome. We will make it even if I have to get in harness too. But swimming is not a good thing. Let's stay off the thin ice. Got that Utah, Alto?"

e-Mail: *Greetings Chris, Lots and lots of prayers from Mancelona, MI.*

I have been conversing with your Mother in the past few days...and sent emails to your Dad leading up to the Iditarod.

This email in particular sums up the respect and admiration I have for what you are doing. You are an amazing young man! You are also our link to this race. Your latest entry brought a smile. Your Dad's spirits were revived—what a blessing. I hope he can feel the power of prayer coming his way! The dogs sound jazzed! What an accomplishment!

I'm so proud of your Dad. I wish I were there to see the smile on his face as he pulls into the finish line. Oh, and good luck finding your Mom. I bet she will find you first! Mothers are like that. Sherry Sutherby (Russ and Sherry from www.lastchancekennel. com)

Chris, March 20: After two days in Nome, all of the mushers from Michigan have come in except my dad. There are relatively few spectators here in Nome now that the first group of mushers has come in. There are still several touron (a cross between tourist and moron) things to do, but most of them require cash. I have gotten really good at waiting around, but these last two days have really been long.

Al and Ed came in yesterday. Both are all smiles, and glad that it is over.

Jim and Hartley: Hartley, a 60 lb 2-year old male and named after my Dad, never had a slack tug for over a 1000 miles. But when Hartley looks back at you he is telling you something important. About 30 miles out of Nome I noticed a pair of eyes reflecting back from my headlamp. It was Hartley. I stopped the team and checked him out. I found no snow in his booties, no sore shoulders or wrists. I squatted in front of him to have a talk. He put his head on my knee and said he was tired, very tired. I disconnected his tug line to give him a rest while running. We moved on.

About 10 miles out of Nome Hartley began looking back again, this time in desperation. I stopped the team and checked him again. This time I pulled his booties off and gave him a little lamb fat to eat. I asked him if he wanted to ride into Nome in the sled bag. He didn't but was very tired.

One mile out of Nome, Hartley began staggering. I stopped the team for about 10 minutes. He stood motionless with his head low but wagged when I called his name. I showed him the lights of Nome across the ice covered sea. We pressed on. I was hoping he could make it. As we neared the snow ramp up onto Front Street he was staggering badly. I yelled, "Hartley, let's go!" With his last strength he tightened the neckline and pulled up the ramp onto Front Street. He ran down Front Street and across the finish line like he wasn't even tired. But he was one tired puppy. We all were very tired puppies.

Up the Snow Ramp to Front Street in Nome

Chris, March 21: After 13 days, 20 hours, 15 minutes, my Dad crossed the finish line of the Iditarod Sled Dog Race. He was thrilled, to say the least. I am happy for him. He has put more on the line in the last 6 months than most of us have our entire lives. I am really happy to see him, but I am even happier to see my dogs, especially Reba, Hartley, and Stormy. I raised them from their birth, and they are almost like children.

When he came in he was slightly disoriented. He said he started at 7:30 this morning, only to be reminded that it was 5:15 in the morning. I gave him bit of a hard time about coming in just as the bars closed. I will have to write more as soon as the banquet is over and things have settled.

Jim at Finish of Iditarod '04

Jim, Nome: At the finish line I'd have been happy even if nobody showed up. But to my delight there were a number of folks there! In fact it seemed quite crowded. I was touched and appreciated deeply them getting out of bed at 5am to come to the finish line to see a trail-weary team and musher finish. Jennifer had flown back from home to be there. Al, Jim, Ed, and others were all there. I was somewhat disoriented but otherwise feeling fine. It had been a 9-10 hour run from White Mountain.

The finish line was a satisfying time for me; no ecstasy, just a subdued and deep satisfaction. But in that place of lights, people and noise, I was frequently casting glances at my dogs to be sure they were still OK. They were more than OK! They were happy to be getting special attention from Chris and hugs from Jennifer. Hartley was resting on the snow and was just fine. I went to them and thanked each dog; a deep and heartfelt thanks. I am unable to find words to adequately describe my gratitude to those dogs. All too quickly, I was ready to take them to the Iditarod Nome Dog Lot and care for them.

We secured the dogs on a picket and gave them each a big pile of straw. Their harnesses were removed for the first time in almost two weeks. We gave them a good rubdown. They were fed with the best, given a warm blanket, and helped to burrow into the straw. They deserved it. They had earned it the old fashioned way with a lot of hard work. They had accomplished what few dare

As Jen, Chris and I started to walk away toward Fat Freddie's restaurant, about a block away, I had to stop. I just couldn't walk away from my dogs. I had been with them for so long and through so much it seemed wrong to walk away, without them. I gazed back at the sleeping dogs for a moment, and then forced myself to turn and walk away.

After the best breakfast I've ever had, I told Chris and Jen we needed to check on the dogs before we went to our hosts. I desperately needed a shower and nap, but I also was suffering withdrawal; dog withdrawal. I wanted to see them. We walked back to the dog lot where they were sleeping, looking much like 'puddles of fur on straw'. I thought of sleeping there on the sled with them but didn't dare mention it to anybody. Standing among my dogs with my wife and son, on the Bering Sea coast in Nome, it finally sank in: Iditarod was over for us.

No longer a dream, it was real. With one of those rare gifts of life, the overwhelming feeling of 'it's so good to be alive', with tears, I walked away from my sleeping dogs.

A Good Day, A Very Good Day!

e-Mail: Jennifer, Congratulations to Jim and team for his finish of Iditarod 2004! What an awesome feeling it must have been for Jim as he crossed under the arch in Nome. Brings chills to think he undertook and accomplished such a feat! Great Job! Lynne

Jim: I hadn't looked at my leg since injury, intentionally. I had tried to control swelling by keeping it tightly wrapped in my boot and bibs by cinching down the Velcro closures. It was still very swollen but the coloration from bleeding down around the ankle and the lower calf was already partially absorbed. Jennifer thinks the doctor will want to have an MRI to determine if surgical reattachment is needed. Otherwise walking on level ground the pain is minimal but the leg is weak. I think the healing had been accelerated by the miles of use and anti-inflammatory drugs.

Jen and Chris looked at me in disbelief when I told them of the blurred vision and numb hand. They understood when I struggled to read the menu at the restaurant in Nome. The vision was improving but the hand was totally without feeling.

e-Mail: Dear Jennifer: Been following Jim on the internet, what a tremendous undertaking for you all to complete the Iditarod. I was rooting and praying for him every day. CONGRATULATIONS!!!!!!!!
God Bless, Fred & Lurinda Fletcher

Chris, March 23: My dad was really fortunate to finish when he did. He was able to care for his dogs, eat a massive breakfast, take a nap, and wake up in time for the finishers' banquet. What a feast! Fresh fruit and veggies, roast beef, halibut, and beans, just to start. I wound up eating two whole plates of food, and I didn't even get to try everything. While I was eating, Ed, Al, Jim, and my dad began swapping stories. I couldn't remember half of them if I tried, but I still shake my head and wonder how on earth all four of them survived. Now that my dad is sitting here, in Nome, he is able to look back and recognize how he was reacting to the extreme fatigue he faced on the trail. He can recognize what he was going through now that he has had some good sleep, but he is quick to point out how insurmountable it seemed at the time. I don't know how my dad made it from the start to the finish, but he did.

The dogs are in the Nome dog lot, patiently waiting for their plane ride out of here. My dad and I are waiting too, but nowhere near as patiently. Since the finish, we have been getting ready to leave for Anchorage. The other Michigan Mushers left already, I can't say I blame them. I am stuck here with my dad taking care of three teams for the next two days. I don't mind. The other handlers took care of our dogs in Anchorage so that I could travel the trail. The only problem is the lady who is running the dog lot. She has relatively little to do, so she seems to find minor problems and almost panics over them. That and she seems so lonely that as soon as she sees me she wants to start a conversation. I have yet to feed the dogs without spending 15 minutes trying to get her to stop talking. I will have another update later; my dad wants his computer back.

Chris, March 25: The sea ice here is something else. It is a primal landscape. It changes by the hour; you can hear its groaning and crunching underneath your feet. There is nothing like it. Standing on the edge of Lake Superior when it's frozen is the closest you can get, and it still doesn't compare. It scares me, to be honest. If you can imagine an arctic hell, the frozen sea ice is it.

We begin our journey home today. The long journey home is something that I am not looking forward to. I don't mind going home; I look forward to that, the drive is what gets me. With the side trips we are taking, the trip will be in excess of 4000 miles and very, very long emotionally. The trip here was only a little shorter, but I was preparing gear and supplies for the race. There is nothing to prepare for on the way home, just waiting for the trip to be over. When I take off on the plane from Nome to Anchorage today I will begin trying to sleep as much as possible. I will need it if my dad wants to compress our schedule to meet his imaginary deadline. Traveling with a 'type A' personality can be a challenge

Those who have read my father's training journal may remember that my father's father was in love with Alaska. He read every book, newspaper article, and magazine related to Alaska. He watched the homesteaders move to Alaska and wanted to go. I'm not sure why he never did, but I am sure that he couldn't get enough of this great land. By running the Iditarod, my dad became intimately connected with Alaska. As best I knew my grandfather, and from stories my dad told, my grandfather would be envious. It is as though my father was following his father's dream.

In the same sense, I was fortunate enough to follow my father's dream. Instead of waiting until I was older, I was able to literally follow my father along the trail. This journey has been an awakening for me. I have learned more about the important things in life, like who I am, what I believe, and what is important to me, in the last month than any amount of school can provide.

***

Jim, Looking Back

Never Alone: Although much of the Iditarod trail is hundreds of miles away from anything, I never felt alone. The relationship with the dogs is something not easily described. They are always talking to each other and to you. Body language and eye contact are the most recognizable forms of communication. We talked all the way to Nome.

Beyond My Limits: Much of life is about understanding your limits and operating within them. I think running the Iditarod is a step beyond. It is about how to manage yourself when you have pushed well beyond your perceived limits, physically and mentally, for sustained periods of time. The effects of fatigue, the demands on my body in the cold, the punishment of driving a sled across hundreds of miles of rough back country, all came together to take a tremendous toll. Managing under these conditions could only be practiced under the real conditions. This part wasn't a whole lot of fun but I did learn a lot about myself.

Weight Loss: I started the Iditarod at a tight 34 inch waist. In 13 days I became a loose 32. I had to buy a belt in Nome to hold up my borrowed 32 inch waist jeans. I ate everything I could find at the checkpoints! I hallucinated about eating sticks of margarine and bacon grease sandwiches. We had packed over 8000 calories for each day of travel. The problem was I didn't test my food under trail conditions. When it didn't work at first I was already too tired to troubleshoot. The highs and lows of the trip correlate exactly to my severe calorie deprivation. Of all the things done right in preparation for this event, this single item nearly scuttled the effort by amplifying the effects of fatigue and pain.

Sleep Deprivation: I thought I would have a hard time waking after a couple hours sleep, especially after days of chronic fatigue. It was not the case. I was able to drop to sleep almost instantly and usually woke on my own slightly before the time I wanted. This was a nice surprise. I slept on the sled, on straw thrown on the snow, on the floor in the checkpoints, leaning against stairs and once with my legs in across a busy doorway. I didn't try sleeping while the sled was moving but I did tie my wrist to the sled on the Yukon River out of Ruby just in case I dozed off.

The main effect of the sleep schedule was paranoia. I began thinking about leaving the checkpoints dwelling on all the problems and getting worked up. I recognized this early but wasn't able to overcome it. This is so unlike me it was a surprise.

Hallucinations: Sleep deprivation combined with exposure often results in hallucinations. Mushers expect them and entertain by telling stories of them. Hallucinations are different than dreams. They are real, so very real. You can't tell them apart from reality. You live them with all your senses and emotions. In every sense they are real, no fooling, they are better than real. Somehow you can be aware you are hallucinating but that doesn't remove the reality! I've never experienced anything like it.

I think it was on the run across Norton Sound from Shaktoolik to Koyuk. It was cold. I was wearing everything

I had, it was at night, the wind was drifting the snow across the tracks, and the lights of Koyuk were tiny specks on a so distant horizon. There was no moon, no aurora, just black, big black. I was following the reflection of the trail markers as if in a trance. Once or twice I moved the beam of my headlamp to the side only to see nothing, nothing but more sea ice. This was a bleak place. All that mattered was getting through it.

I spotted a package of Parkay margarine on the ice and scooped it up as I passed. What a find! I had been calorie deprived most of the time for the last week and half and I needed fat, lots of fat. I opened the first cube and stuffed it into my mouth. It was wonderful. I loved the taste; I even loved how it stuck to the roof of my mouth. I marveled at my good fortune. Who would have ever thought I would find a package of Parkay out on the ice 30 miles from anything. I licked the last of it off my teeth, enjoying it. In my haste to get to the next cube, I crumpled the paper and threw it on the ice. Instantly, guilt ridden, I stopped the team so I could retrieve the litter so carelessly thrown onto this pristine wilderness. But nowhere was it to be seen. I thought the wind may had blown it away.

So without delay, I looked on the top of the sled bag where I had deposited the remaining cubes. I couldn't find them. I looked, alongside the sled, checked my pockets, I even unzipped the sled bag to double check inside.

With the team stopped, somewhere on the sea ice before Koyuk, the realization that this was a hallucination fell on me. At first I felt silly and apologized to the dogs, then I felt angry for loosing my Parkay. Then I felt even sillier because I knew I didn't loose the Parkay, it was a hallucination. But it was real, so real I can still taste it. It was hard to let go. But we had to move on, forever moving on.

Some time later during the same run the hallucination took me to a different setting. I was home from school, about 7 years old, standing in my grandmother's kitchen with my chin just about counter height, watching, smelling, while Granny slathered a slice of homemade bread with bacon grease. The farm kitchen always had a crock near the stove to gather fryings and there was nothing better than bacon grease on Granny's homemade bread. Sometimes she would let me put honey on it too. Life was good, the way it should be. I raised both of my hands to receive the monster slice of bread. I damn near fell backwards off the moving dogsled! The hallucination was instantly replaced by the gut wrenching fear of loosing my team on the sea ice. I felt cheated by missing out on Granny's bread, but having both hands on the handlebar, still in control of my team was a great solace. The lights of Koyuk seemed a little closer although they had been in sight for hours. It was cold, very cold, a killing cold.

I still felt cheated. Why couldn't the hallucination have lasted until I finished the bacon grease sandwich? It was real, so real, I can still almost smell the cold bacon grease.

So it is in the Alaskan wilderness with the mentally limited Iditarod musher.

It Makes You Wonder: Six months after Iditarod '04, I awoke one morning with the knowledge that I had regained a piece of memory of the '04 Iditarod race heretofore not available to me. Now that is strange, real strange. I had wondered both privately and openly about seemingly inconsistent facts. Why had I run for 14 hours straight from Cripple to Ruby? It was only 65 miles. It just didn't make sense.

My race plan called for a camp of 4-5 hours between

Cripple and Ruby. I had in my drop bags the needed dog food for the extra feeding and dog snacks. Depending on conditions on the trail I could have chosen to run straight through or to rest. But, my memory did not include any stop. But I did stop! I now remember it in detail.

I stopped about 4 hours out of Cripple in a little wooded gully where the wind was blocked and the afternoon sun would help warm us. I fed, and checked dog feet, then settled in for a nap on the sled. My leg had been noticeably hurting more, and was throbbing with every heartbeat. I assumed the swelling was getting worse or perhaps it was that I was taking no more pain meds. So I planned to reverse my sleeping position on the sled and place my inured leg on the sled handlebar at a higher elevation than my head. Now this is a goofy looking thing to do.

I awakened when a snowmobile engine stopped alongside of us. A man and a woman were sitting on the snowmobile just a few feet away curiously looking at me. When I said this was the way I always sleep on the sled they just looked at each other and changed the subject. I asked where they were going, knowing there was nothing for a hundred miles back up the trail? They said they were going to Caribou camp to commune with nature. OK, that made as much sense as my comment.

A half hour later a second snowmobile stopped, again curious. This time it was a man and a teenage boy looking for a man and a woman. The man said his son had run off with the wife of a village man. He hoped to find them and return the woman before there was trouble. I told him what I had learned earlier. He roared off.

An hour later the two snowmobiles drove by in the opposite direction and waved happily. It seemed like a soap opera scene, Alaskan style. But it was time for us to move on. There were serious hills to climb before Ruby and I was in no shape to enjoy them.

But, this very clear memory had been unavailable until now. I don't understand.

The Dogs: They performed marvelously. There were 10 in harness at the finish. I was thrilled that no dogs were dropped because of the common shoulder or wrist soreness; tough dogs. This is even more remarkable because my left hand numbness greatly limited my ability to massage the dogs. But the whole team came down with an intestinal virus slowing us dramatically from Ophir through Cripple and into Ruby. I estimate we lost close to 24 hours but all dogs recovered and were able to continue.

Finish: We finished in 13 days and within our target of 12-14 days. To my surprise that turned out to be late in the last quartile. Two years ago it was slightly behind mid field. If you go back as few as a dozen years or so, 13 days could give a top 10 position and occasionally a top 5 and a shot at winning. You need a solid 10 day finish to be in the top 20 now.

Tunes: I am about as musical as a rock. But three tunes kept coming to me and playing in my head. I never did know all the words but I tried making up words to sing to the dogs. It helped them and minimized my boredom. They were, "One Day at a Time" by Cristy Lane, "Some Days are Diamonds" by John Denver, and "Running on Empty" by Jackson Browne.

Hurt: After running much of Iditarod injured, I have a new and deep respect for athletes who often 'play hurt'. I also think that it was an awesome feat for Doug Swingley to win Iditarod after suffering rib injuries at the start.

Running a large dog team on the Iditarod Trail is a whole body sport. There is no way you can do much to favor an injury; you have to use it, hurting or not.

The hamstring I injured runs up the rear of the inner thigh and ends just above the hip joint; one of those places that you can't massage in public. Low level pain was constant but would spike when I had to pedal or run a step or two to help the dogs. It felt like someone was ramming a screw driver into my upper thigh/hip joint. Although I tried to not groan audibly, there were more than a few times the startled dogs looked back when I groaned in anguish. This was a nasty injury.

MVP Team Dog goes to Hartley. He pulled all the way to and up Topkok, but was pretty tired getting in to Nome at the end of that 77 Mile run. On command he gave the last of his strength running up the snow ramp onto Nome's Front Street.

MVP Lead Dog goes to Alto. He suffered a major bite wound to his front foot two weeks before the start. He had two punctures going completely through the foot with one pad split open in three directions. Hoping for fast healing, Chris and I reconstructed his pad with super glue and mole skin. We changed bandages several times a day. He started the Iditarod with his pad still held together with superglue. He never limped once and ran 1100 miles, much of it in lead.

Alto, One Tough Dog

MVP Rookie goes to Reba. She is a 2 year old female, Hartley's sister, and Whitney's favorite. When I was having trouble with leaders in the heat of the day before Ruby, I tried her in lead. She led for 300-400 miles alongside of several others.

Three Rookie Mushers from Michigan Finish Iditarod '04: All four mushers are from Michigan, three of them rookies, finished Iditarod '04; a grand accomplishment. Much of the success is attributable directly to Al Hardman's generous coaching, advice, and encouragement

Jim Warren, Ed Stielstra, Jim Conner, Al Hardman

Trail Delirium:
The overwhelming fatigue of the trail is impossible to describe adequately. You have to experience it to know. After days and nights of exposure to the cold and wind combined with severe sleep deprivation, my mental state started to crumble. Fatigue became my master. It twisted reality, altered time, and distorted, no, almost destroyed my memory. There was no way to know before hand how much or little I was going to be affected. In my altered state I become my own worst enemy. Sometimes I think only a fool would intentionally tempt fate this way. Thus it is with the Iditarod musher.

Time is moving on! On the trail in the dark of night my world shrank into the tiny space lighted by my headlamp. Its length was about as long as a dog team and about half as wide. There was nothing else in my world; nothing else mattered. The hours and hours of silence were broken only by the squeaking of the sled runners on the cold snow and the soft panting of the dogs. The drifting snow and wind intruded. Occasionally the aurora, moon or stars reminded me there may be more to my tiny world than what showed in my headlamp. The dogs were running, forever running ahead. We were moving, going somewhere but not always sure where. The dogs were moving ahead, insanely, forever moving ahead, trotting and loping, through the artic darkness. Time moves on.

Instantly it had become full daylight; no dawn transition, it seemed. My world had expanded to an almost unimaginable size with mountains, hills, tundra, and sea ice as far as I could see. We, the team and I, shrank smaller than a spec of dust in a universe of white, wind and cold. I was sure I'd stopped moving, sled runners frozen to the ice, trapped in this big, so very big valley. I looked down at the snow just to be sure I was really moving ahead. The dogs were always moving ahead, insanely, forever moving ahead with no hope of getting past that artic valley.

But the big bright world was exciting. There was a lot of room to dream big dreams, and imagine great things. The world was without limit. It seemed warmer too.

I was living in the small space of a moving dog sled. I was trapped by the fear that one step sideways or rearward would change everything; eternal loss! My team would leave me alone, a horrible thought. So I remained trapped on the eternally moving dogsled. The dogs had no mercy, they kept moving, forever, insanely moving ahead. I loved those dogs. I feared being without them, alone, on the trail. Time moves on.

Memory is a strange feature of a human brain. You consult it to recall where you have come from most recently. You can, with your memory, consult your race plan and know where you are going. If you made a mental note of the time of departure from the last checkpoint, and still from memory, added the expected travel time, you can with some precision forecast when you should arrive at the next checkpoint. So goes the technical discussion of how memory can serve the Iditarod musher. The reality is often quite different.

I looked at my watch and then couldn't remember why. Then I vaguely remembered we were on a 7 hour run with expected arrival time at 11am; or was it an 11 hour run arriving at 7, am or pm? What time did I leave the last checkpoint? It was dark when I left. Or was that the previous checkpoint?

Yes my memory was on an elastic timeline, sometimes no timeline, just random fragmented events. I worried about it at first fearing I might miss a checkpoint. Then I decided to be very good at following the trail markers. I was running from one trail marker to the next; thousands of little journeys through the artic night and unending cold. The dogs kept moving ahead, insanely, forever moving ahead. Time moves on.

In the checkpoint the dogs dropped on the straw bed they so richly deserved, earned the old fashioned way, with hard work. They eat a good meal, no a great meal, the equivalent of a family Christmas dinner for humans, they get checked out by the best vets in the world, and then drop off to sleep. I am still moving. The checkpoint routine is a well practiced procedure and consists of hooking down the team, removing dog booties, dropping straw, starting the alcohol cooker, melting snow, mixing and feeding the food to the dogs, prep a future dog meal, repack the sled for departure, and finally, for me, food and rest. On the straw or on the sled in my sleeping bag, sleep is more like a coma than good wholesome unconscious sleep. Yes, my body was resting but my mind was moving, never stopping, like the dogs moving ahead, insanely moving, forever moving ahead. After 1-2 hours I am cold, up again, moving, feeding, booting dog feet, and preparing the team to run, moving always moving. Then, ready to leave, it starts again. The dogs are running, moving ahead with speed and enthusiasm after their rest. They pick out the trail markers in the artic darkness and begin following them. The cold wind was biting and looking for openings in my garments to suck away my life. But the dogs were moving ahead, insanely, forever moving ahead into the wind driven snow. My world shrank again to the tiny size of a headlamp beam. Nothing mattered except what was in the beam. Time moves on.

Over the miles and miles of the artic night my mind wandered. I once had a life, far away and long ago. I had a home with a wife and children on a Christmas tree farm in Michigan. It was warm and moist there, green too. Insects swarmed after the summer rains. There seemed to be no connection from then to now, like a fragmented dream. How did it get this way? The dogs kept moving ahead, trotting, panting, insanely, moving ahead, through the artic silence, miles and miles of complete silence.

A moment ago it was night, full dark, no moon, only the aurora to entertain. Instantly it is full daylight. Through a light snowfall I can see buildings on the horizon. But we are far from Elim.

Suddenly over the crest of a small hill a speeding snowmobile appeared heading straight toward us. Disaster was imminent! The driver deftly threw the machine into a power slide, missed, but showered us with ice and snow. Hartley spun around in his harness and barked in anger at the departing snowmobile. I stopped the team to gather our composure. Together, alive and healthy, a man and his dogs celebrated life, life preserved; life, a fragile thing in this great land of snow, ice, and the never ending cold. Time moves on.

Elim was different the last time I was here. Then it was bigger, more inviting, better. I was the fortunate traveling partner of Charlie Eshbach. Almost a folk hero to my family, he is a man with a special way of telling a story and the ability to warm the heart. My son Christopher is traveling along the trail with Charlie this trip. I am almost envious.

I think of Chris often. I can almost feel his presence along the trail. I imagine him standing in the checkpoint watching the teams arrive. I can see him connected to the internet updating our journals. In Galena, the lady running the checkpoint asked me to tell him that he was invited to return to help with a future checkpoint and she expressed great respect for him. She made my day. Then in Unalakleet, down on the river ice in the dark of the checkpoint, I was startled when a big shadow walked over to me and excitedly shouted, "Mr. Warren," and then bear-hugged me pulling my feet off the ground. The voice sounded strangely familiar through the mental fog of fatigue but I couldn't identify the person. Then it hit me, it was Chris! What a boost. Time moves on.

People are kind to the fatigue-embattled Mushers. In Nulato I watched a very tired lady veterinarian mix up a triple batch of macaroni and cheese. I may have been staring unknowingly, not at the woman, but at the mac and cheese. She ate just a tiny amount and offered the rest to me. I wolfed down the entire pot. As she left to check a team, she said, "I am glad you enjoyed the mac and cheese." I replied, "You have no idea how much I enjoyed it." She looked at me and smiled. I was wrong, she knew. She had looked into my soul with knowing eyes, and knew. Time moves on.

Filled with apprehension I tended the dogs in the dark behind a building in Kaltag. After days of running on the Yukon River a critical obstacle lay ahead, the climb out of Kaltag on the portage trail to Unalakleet. With my injured leg I feared I would not be able to make the climb.

My overdeveloped personal drive pushed me on. There was nothing in me, not a fiber in my body, that would let me quit voluntarily. No way! I've lived my life holding to the standard: If I can still hold up my head, if I can still walk, then keep moving; to work, to school, whatever.

We were moving ahead one checkpoint at a time, one hill at a time, and sometimes in desperation, a much, much shorter objective. Step by step, hour by hour, mile by mile and day by day, we moved ahead.

***

See ongoing Web Journal at:
www.warren-enterprises.com

***

Give books as a gift. Order at:
www.amazon.com

***